LIVING WELL
with ADHD

TERRY HUFF, LCSW

Forword by Melissa Orlov, best-selling author of
The ADHD Effect on Marriage
and
The Couple's Guide to Thriving with ADHD

Book Design and Layout: Babs Kall

Book Cover Design: www.ElmStreetDesignStudio.net

Specialty Press, Inc.
300 Northwest 70th Avenue, Suite 102
Plantation, Florida 33317
(954) 792-8100 • (800) 233-9273

Printed in the United States of America

ISBN 978-1-937761-24-0

Library of Congress Cataloging-in-Publication Data

Names: Huff, Terry M., 1949- author.
Title: Living well with ADHD / Terry M. Huff.
Description: Plantation, Florida : Specialty Press, Inc., [2016]
Identifiers: LCCN 2015045721 (print) | LCCN 2015046817 (ebook) |
    ISBN 9781937761240 (paperback) | ISBN 9781937761271 () |
    ISBN 9781937761288 | ISBN 9781937761257
Subjects: LCSH: Attention-deficit hyperactivity disorder | BISAC: BODY,
    MIND & SPIRIT / Meditation.
Classification: LCC RJ506.H9 H84 2016 (print) | LCC RJ506.H9 (ebook) |
    DDC 618.92/8589–dc23
LC record available at http://lccn.loc.gov/2015045721

Author's Note

In the interest of privacy, many of the names in this book are pseudonyms, and some of the details have been modified to mask identities. Some individuals who are identified encouraged me to use their actual names.

I encourage you to read the book all the way through to the end. I'm painfully aware that individuals with ADHD don't always finish what they start, and I'm guilty of that. So, I wrote a book that you can finish! Its manageable length is by design, and I don't want you to miss the last chapters that will point you in a direction and help you achieve your goals.

I have included pages in the back of the book for you to make notes if you wish. President Harry Truman was known for underlining and writing in the margins of books. It's a good idea!

Preface

From the moment I read the first words of *Living Well with ADHD* by Terry Huff, until I put it down to reflect on its many important messages, my brain was mesmerized by the powerful words, stories, metaphors, and deep insight Terry has artfully and eloquently conveyed in his highly engaging and empowering book. Terry's book will not only capture your entire focus, but provide you with a powerful, positive perspective that will inspire you to learn how to successfully manage your ADHD. It is also an excellent resource for those supporting someone with ADHD. It clearly will help them understand what adults with ADHD experience with the invisible challenges of their ADHD every day.

Living Well with ADHD was written to provide all of its readers with a greater, more in-depth understanding that ADHD does not mean you're broken — or less than — but you possess a unique brain wiring. Once you understand how your unique brain wiring works and embrace it, you can create many of the possibilities which have been buried inside of your heart for many many years. You will gain the confidence that comes with knowing what works with your ADHD so you can passionately pursue opportunities.

The stories, the strategies, and the personal and professional experience Terry brings to this book will shine the light on the internal brilliance you've always possessed, but without having given yourself permission to proceed. This is an inspiring and transformative book that will empower you to shift your focus from problems and weakness to possibilities and strengths. It will encourage you to pursue opportunities in a realistic and achievable manner.

Once you read it, your life with ADHD will never be the same!

David Giwerc, Founder and president of the ADD Coach Academy and author of the groundbreaking book Permission to Proceed: the Keys to Creating a life of Passion, Purpose and Possibilities *(www.addca.com).*

Praise for Terry Huff and *Living Well with ADHD*

Not since Dr. Edward Hallowell and Dr. John Ratey's 'Distraction' series have I read such an empowering book on ADHD, and I'm excited about it! *Living Well with ADHD* is upbeat and informative. Fun. Realistic. Hopeful. Useful.

> *Melissa Orlov, marriage consultant to couples impacted by ADHD and award-winning author of* The ADHD Effect on Marriage *and* The Couples Guide to Thriving with ADHD

Terry Huff, expertly and with a personal, touching voice, describes the various ways to tap into inner resources for awareness and self-directedness. Rooted in mindfulness practice applied to daily living, these strategies can be liberating, healing and surprising—showing what's possible, often beyond our own expectations.

> *Lidia Zylowska M.D. Co-founder of UCLA Mindful Awareness Research Center and author of* The Mindfulness Prescription for Adult ADHD

This book is simply awesome!! *Living Well with ADHD* is thoughtful and encouraging, just like the author. Adults who want to transform their cognitive differences from liabilities into gifts will want to use this book as a guide. His years of counseling and personal experience are apparent as he leads us to those insights about creativity and relationships that will help you thrive.

> *David Owens, Ph.D., Professor of Management, Vanderbilt University Graduate School of Management Author of* Creative People Must Be Stopped!

This book provides a positive perspective that will inspire and empower you. It is also an excellent resource for those supporting someone with ADHD. This is a book you have to get today because once you read it, your life with ADHD will never be the same! I highly recommend *Living Well with ADHD* by Terry Huff.

> *David Giwerc, Founder and president of the ADD Coach Academy and author of Permission to Proceed*

This book is a must read for anyone with ADHD who wants to live a more full and mindful life. Terry's personal experience and expertise shine through in every chapter. He skillfully guides the reader through applying the principles of mindfulness in daily living that will greatly enhance their ability to live well with ADHD.

Lisa Ernst, Meditation Teacher and Founder
of One Dharma Nashville

Dedication

In memory of:

My parents, Honor and Glenn Huff, who believed in me
and loved me unconditionally

My mother-in-law, Mary Gene Field, an educator who
respected all of her students and taught them to love learning.

Daniel Rochester and Andrew Burns, and to
the continuing commitment of their compassionate fathers
who have helped countless individuals with ADHD
and continue to do so

Acknowledgements

I am forever grateful to my father, who was the most patient and loving man I've ever known, and to my playful mother, who refused to grow up. My mother tricked me into believing that I could be anything I wanted to be, and my father taught me to love my work and live a useful life.

I owe so much to my thoughtful and resilient wife, who has lived with my ADHD for decades and still loves me. Despite my reluctance to grow up, my marriage matured. Anne knows that I care about her even when I don't recall what she told me thirty minutes ago. Because of her compassionate frankness, I understand how my ADHD symptoms affect her, and she knows that I share her concerns. She wholeheartedly encouraged this project, despite knowing how much attention I would be giving to my laptop.

I am grateful to my spirited daughter, Lindsay, who has been a bright light in my life from day one. I'm proud to be the father of this competent, funny, and loving young woman, and I'm envious of her processing speed. She completed her master's degree as I was completing this book. Lindsay has tolerated my ADHD with love and mercy.

Thanks to my big brother, who still marvels at the many mindless things I did in our youth, but always with respect. I marvel at his uncanny ability to remember jokes and punch lines.

A special shout-out to ADDNashville! No other experience in my career has allowed me to learn so much in such a mutual process—and in real time—as being a "player/coach" with this support group. The willingness of members to expose their vulnerabilities, share their successes, commit to the group process, contribute to the collective wisdom, and support each other's efforts has inspired and enlightened me. Their creative ideas for coping strategies have helped many.

Thanks to my friend Jim Fuller, life coach and career specialist, for encouraging me to write a book. My songwriting had been costing me money and earning me none.

Thanks to Phyllis Dorn, my friend, business partner, and the best psychotherapist I know, for always being supportive and honest. I am especially grateful for her kindness to my ADHD clients who occasionally show up in the waiting room on my day off, or when I'm on vacation.

Thanks to Sarah Eckstein, who took time from working on her dissertation to help me with some editing and technical advice. Sarah grew up surrounded by ADHD in her family and is now researching attitudes toward mindfulness among adults with ADHD.

Thanks to Dr. Rick Rochester, a valued friend and go-to psychiatrist for adults with ADHD, who has been enhancing the lives of my referrals for twenty years. And to Dr. David Burns, who diagnosed my ADHD in midlife. Both physicians understand ADHD and care deeply about their patients.

A special thanks to Editor Dave. Dave Carew has become more than my editor. I'm pleased to count him among my cherished friends. He knows more about the Beatles and baseball than anyone I know. His understanding of the business of writing, editing, and publishing gave me the confidence to start this project and keep moving forward.

Thanks to my life-long California friends, who have always been accepting and supportive. Dr. Paul Carlo and Cecily Kahn are model social workers who have done much good for a lot of people throughout their long careers. Thanks to Dr. Robert Fischer and Anne LaRiviere—pioneers in helping young adults transition into independent living—at the Optimal Performance Institute in Woodland Hills, California.

Mike Himelstein was the success story in my song lyric writing class at UCLA in 1978. I'm grateful for his continuing friendship and always inspired by his creativity, accomplishments, and sick sense of humor. He gives laughter generously. Thanks to the late Buddy Kaye, our lyric writing teacher and successful writer of "songs for all time" (In 2015, Bob Dylan released his recording of a Buddy Kaye song that was a major hit for Frank Sinatra seventy years earlier). Buddy inspired me to create and gave me tools to work with. Most of all, he believed in me.

Thanks to Lisa Ernst, founder of One Dharma Nashville, for enhancing my mindfulness practice and helping me with a meditation workshop for adults with ADHD. And to my old Nashville Zen Center friends, especially Dr. Bill Compton—founder of NZC—who wrote the first textbook on positive psychology, which inspired parts of this book. I'm forever grateful to two meditation teachers who woke me up to aspects of life that I would have missed without their influence—Sandy Gentei Stewart, North Carolina Zen Center's first Osho and Abbot; and Trudy Goodman, founder of Insight LA in Santa Monica and co-founder of the Institute for Meditation and Psychothcrapy in Buston.

I cannot say enough about the contributions of Melissa Orlov, the expert on ADHD and marriage. Melissa encouraged me and was unbelievably generous with helpful advice. I had to throw away an outline for the first book I was planning to write—for ADHD couples—after reading *The ADHD Effect on Marriage*. Melissa Orlov had already said it all, so well and so clearly, in her important book. I recommend her books to all couples living with ADHD in the relationship.

Thanks to Dr. Harvey Parker—author, psychotherapist, co-founder of CHADD, and founder of Specialty Press—for being so committed to helping families attempting to live well with ADHD and for believing in my book. Thanks to Babs Kall for being so kind and skillful in designing the layout of the book and to Rick Schroeppel for designing a colorful and inspiring cover.

A heartfelt thanks to all my dear friends for being who you are and letting me be me. Your support during this project is just one of many ways you have demonstrated your acceptance, kindness, and generosity. I'm very fortunate.

Contents

Foreword by Melissa Orlov

ADHD is funny…and it's not. Chapter Seven's title captures it in a nutshell. But how to deal with the conflicting emotions and roller coaster experiences you (and your partner and family) may have about ADHD? If you have a sense of humor, living with ADHD can be funny…but it is never *always* funny…and sometimes it's downright tragic. You have to be able to deal with ADHD in all of its forms and experiences. Up, down, and sideways.

Through it all, those with ADHD (and those who love them) must find the inner strength and wherewithal to figure out how to best succeed in a world that places high value on efficiency, orderliness, speaking concisely, and knowing (or at least thinking you know!) just where you are going. That, of course, doesn't sound a whole lot like ADHD to anyone who has dealt with it.

The world needs the insights, energy, creativity and "wild and crazy thinking" of adults with ADHD. Most of all, it needs ADHD thinkers and doers who can live with their ADHD well enough that the symptoms don't sidetrack their lives, and the lives of their families.

And that is where mindfulness comes in. Research shows that mindfulness training can significantly help those with ADHD live more happily and more productively. But how? Terry Huff answers that question in *Living Well with ADHD*. He doesn't provide you the step-by-step instructions for starting a mindfulness practice, though he does tell you where to find that. Rather, he sets up the reasons and numerous benefits of mindfulness so that when it's time get to the nuts and bolts stage of practicing, adults with ADHD will have the inspiration needed to stick with it.

Not since Dr. Edward Hallowell and Dr. John Ratey's *Distraction* series have I read such an empowering book on ADHD, and I'm excited about it! *Living Well with ADHD* is upbeat and informative. It repeatedly reframes how one can view ADHD; for example, noting that trying to "stop procrastination"—an inherently negative framing of a common problem—is much less effective than seeking to "improve activation." Upbeat. Lots more fun. Realistic. Hopeful. Useful.

My specialty is working with couples impacted by adult ADHD in one or both partners. In that work I see over and over again how getting stuck in a negative feedback loop, or a negative definition of the problem at hand ("I never have enough time" or "stop procrastinating") inhibits forward progress. Being able to identify and observe one's emotions, including these negative frames, through mindful, *non-judgmental* reflection is just the beginning of what Terry Huff demonstrates can work to dislodge adults with ADHD from negative thinking. He also busts some long-standing and powerfully negative myths about ADHD. He encourages ADDers to accept and find the positives in their ADD-ness. And, perhaps most importantly of all, he explains why it's so important to stop trying to be non-ADHD. He shows why pursuing a goal that is so out of synch with having ADHD will only bring you—and those around you—pain.

This is a message adults with ADHD—and their partners, friends, and family—need to hear. The goal is *not* to try harder to be non-ADHD, but rather to embrace your own special qualities in a way that lets you be you *and live the life you most wish to live.* Terry Huff is not talking about irresponsibly just doing anything. He's talking about honestly and *effectively* being you. Best of all, he explains how—and why—this will work. Huff will convince you why it's so important to start this journey, and will get you going.

Managing ADHD isn't just about mindfulness, of course. Getting the traits of ADHD to work for you, rather than against you, means optimizing treatment in the physiological, behavioral, and interactive spheres—what I call the "three legs of ADHD treatment." Mindfulness fits into that second, behavioral, leg. And it's incredibly meaningful to both the person with the ADHD and to everyone around him or her, because adopting practices of mindfulness results in living a calmer, more intentional life—one in which the adult with ADHD can start to *choose* the directions, emotional responses, and events that best support him or her—rather than be victim to whatever happens to capture one's attention in the moment.

As a person with ADHD, and as a therapist who has helped those with ADHD for many years, Terry Huff is intimately familiar with the challenges, joys, crises, and surprises that adult ADHD brings. His approach is gentle, but it firmly moves you in a new direction. You are, he points out in one example, full of thoughts and a *surplus* of attention to pay to *every single one of them!* But mindfulness also shows you that you are not your thoughts. Thoughts are just thoughts. You are your feelings and actions and, when you develop a habit of mindful attention, you have more control over how to respond to those feelings and follow up on those actions. Mindfulness lets you be you...done well, mindfulness helps you be your "best you."

It is a message of hope. "Encouragement changes lives," writes Huff, and "criticism makes people want to give up." I couldn't agree more. *Living Well with ADHD* offers a specific path to a happier, more fulfilling life for ADHD adults and those who love them. Thank you, Terry, for this wonderful addition to the literature on how to live with ADHD. It is an inspiration!

Melissa Orlov, marriage consultant to couples impacted by ADHD and award-winning author. Her website is at www.ADHDmarriage.com.

Introduction

Maria was the first adult I ever diagnosed with ADHD. A bright and capable forty-year-old divorced mother of two, she was so overwhelmed by her life and so intense in her presentation, I would be exhausted just twenty minutes into a psychotherapy session. She would sit forward on the edge of her chair and talk at a pace I could hardly follow, and with enough energy to drain me of *my* energy.

One day, I decided to help her put on the brakes, as much for me as for her. "Maria, would you please sit all the way back in your chair," I said. "Just take a deep breath, and see if you can slow down a little. You're wearing me out again, and we've just started." She laughed, sat back in her chair, slowed her tempo to a more normal pace, and proceeded with a less pressured presentation. I repeated my request, as needed, to get her to step back from the content of her thoughts and observe the impact of her posture and speech. As I began to suspect ADHD, I asked her a series of questions to explore the possibility. The initial questioning went something like this:

- Do you have a day of the week designated for doing your laundry, or do you wash clothes when you can't find anything clean to wear?

- Do you make a list before you shop for groceries? Do you use coupons?

- Do you know what you have in your bank account?

- What does the back seat of your car look like right now? Your bedroom?

- Do you keep your car's oil changed and its maintenance current?

- Do you use a calendar to keep up with your appointments?

- Do you have difficulty tracking conversations with one person? When interacting with two or three people? When trying to follow a lecture?

- Does your attention drift when reading? Do you have to re-read often because you don't know what you just read?

Maria laughed each time I asked one of these questions. She wondered how I knew to ask them. I learned some things about her attention-management challenges that day.

Maria clipped coupons before shopping for groceries, but didn't use them. When I asked why she didn't use them, she said the large collection of coupons overwhelmed her. She would just close the lid on her little file box and go to the store without them.

"Do you continue to clip and save them?" I asked. Maria laughed and admitted that she continued to clip and save coupons despite never using them. She shopped in no particular order, usually starting on the opposite end of the store from where most shoppers start, and traveling up and down the aisles randomly. It took her twice as long as the average shopper to get her groceries, she said.

Maria's car was always cluttered. One day it caught fire after she had driven too long without an oil change. She never balanced her checkbook and just guessed how much money she had in her account. She washed clothes when she couldn't find any clean clothes to wear.

One day she asked me why she had such difficulty engaging in normal conversations when out with friends at a restaurant or bar. She told me that she couldn't track conversations. Concerned about her hearing, she consulted an audiologist who determined that she had no hearing problem. Her friends followed conversations without effort, she told me. But she was distracted by every conversation that was going on around her, and she missed too much of what her friends were saying. She described it as like being in a glass booth. She was near her friends, but separated from them.

Maria's success with medication for ADHD and depression was so remarkable that she disappeared from therapy for months. Her psychiatrist called me one day to ask when I had last seen her.

"You wouldn't know her," he said. She was working two jobs, managing her finances, and relating to her adolescent daughter more effectively. And he said she was happy.

My own subsequent ADHD diagnosis would further inspire my interest in ADHD and serving others like Maria. I was pleased that my diagnosis qualified me for a support group, and I located one. But I felt unnoticed when I arrived at my first meeting. No one greeted me. A scheduled speaker did not show, and so the leader of the group took it upon himself to make a presentation. I had been listening to clients all day and was not in the mood to listen to a presentation. I would have failed a test on it.

I gave the support group one more try. Again, a speaker was scheduled. The presentation by an audiologist was interesting, but ironically, my auditory processing weakness prevailed. I abandoned the idea of getting the help I wanted from a support group.

Soon afterward, I began to take medication for ADHD and experienced astonishing changes. Not only was I able to create order in my life, I enjoyed the ordering. I was finding that previously boring material was somehow far more interesting to read, and I could comprehend far better. Most surprisingly, I was hearing every word being said in meetings and lectures, which I never thought anyone did. I thought most people, like me, heard about 70 percent of what was said.

In time, I would stop medication, due to another medical problem that precluded taking any stimulant. Discontinuing my ADHD medication forced me to be more resourceful in how to live well with my ADHD brain. Coincidentally, I had just begun practicing Zen meditation with a group. After years of practicing meditation weekly with a group, meditating several times weekly at home, and occasionally attending a three-day retreat, my ability to activate and sustain attention improved tremendously. But then I would focus too well on one activity to the exclusion of my other priorities, and I would lose track of time. When I learned about other forms of meditation practice, I developed the skills to shift my state of awareness better, to unplug from my selectively focused state and return to open awareness where I was more conscious of my environment. I also became more aware of subtle sensations in my body and the places my mind wanted to take me. These practices would later inform me about the difficulty that the ADHD brain has with shifting between selective attention and open awareness. Mindfulness practices didn't "cure" my ADHD, but they enhanced my capacity for living well with it.

About ten years after beginning to specialize in psychotherapy services for adults and adolescents with ADHD, I started an ADHD support group for adults. As I grew in awareness of how ADHD affected marriage, I knew I had to find ways to help ADHD couples learn to partner effectively around the symptoms. Two years after initiating the ADHD support group, I began offering a workshop for couples with ADHD. Some couples I saw had been in marriage therapy for years, often changing therapists, and never quite reaching their goals. Some were on the threshold of divorce after concluding that they had "tried everything."

Each service that I provided directly, or referred my ADHD clients to, inspired me to look further into what else I could do to help this population. With adolescents, I began to attend IEP (individualized education plan) meetings, wherein teachers and administrators would meet with parents and the student to plan how to meet their educational needs. I found that these teenagers often needed an advocate to help teachers understand them and their differences from other students.

I have written this book simply to try to help more people than I can in the world of my private practice, bi-monthly support group, workshop for ADHD couples, presentations to professional and community groups, and networking with providers of other professional services.

I enjoy the process of writing. I spent years reading about writing, imagining writing a book, taking classes in writing, talking about writing, and writing rough outlines for books that I would write. I did everything but write. After I wrote most of this manuscript, I drifted away from my original intention of being helpful and toward becoming a published author. The writing became more difficult. When I got back on track with my original intention—writing to be helpful—I was able to activate again, sustain my attention and effort, and sit still for hours at a time. I'm proud of having done that, if only to illustrate to my ADHD peers that if I can do this, anyone can. You can achieve your life goals as well, whatever they may be. Zen Master D.T. Suzuki told his students, "There is no try; there is only do and not do."

I hope this book will inspire you and teach you ways to move forward:

- from procrastination to activation

- from getting derailed to sustaining your effort

- from inattention to managing attention

- from getting overwhelmed to simplifying your life

- from chaotic activity to mindful action

- from trying to doing

- from living in your head to living your life

This book is not a *disability* perspective. It is an *ability* perspective. If you can go beyond seeing limitations and turn up the lights on possibilities, you will be better able to see your path and drive toward your destination, whatever your life's purpose may be. I want to inspire you to cultivate your abilities, to see your brain as a tool rather than an obstacle, to live your values and actualize your dreams.

Here is a chapter-by-chapter summary of what you will learn in this book:

Chapter One – Who You Are and Who You're Not

Chapter One dispels common misperceptions that you may have about yourself. It begins with what it is like to believe negative comments that parents and teachers made about you, and it presents alternative perspectives. It poses the question: If you are not what your parents and teachers said you are, then who are you? Chapter One challenges you to revisit your perception of who you are and what you can do.

Chapter Two – Wash One Dish: How to Activate Attention and Sustain Effort

I once heard Thomas Brown (Yale University professor and author of *Attention Deficit Disorder: The Unfocused Mind in Children and Adults*) speak about adults with ADHD. He said one of the biggest and most understated problems for adults with ADHD is "activation." Chapter Two frames the activation problem as a neurological feature and presents specific strategies for activating (starting) and sustaining effort (finishing). The metaphor of washing one dish at a time—versus cleaning the kitchen— illustrates a way you can circumvent negative mental activity and transcend the tendency to procrastinate. The chapter focuses on prevention of becoming overwhelmed and sidetracked.

Chapter Three – Attentive Listening and Mindful Speaking

Chapter Three challenges the notion that you are incapable of listening attentively to others, or speaking with mindful consideration of the listener. You may have problems listening attentively and being considerate in speech because you have formed maladaptive habits around your neurological differences. While those differences contribute to tendencies, tendencies do not have to become actualized. Old habits can be supplanted by new, competing habits. Chapter Three addresses how to cultivate and demonstrate mindful consideration of others.

Chapter Four – Bonds and Binds: ADHD in Relationships

Chapter Four illustrates special challenges to couples affected by ADHD in their relationship. It proposes that couple therapy is likely to fail without addressing the impact of the disorder on the partnership. Chapter Four challenges you to step up and share leadership with your relationship partner rather than react as if your partner is a parent. It highlights the need to understand specific effects of ADHD on your partner, and how to rise above defensiveness and resignation in the interest of sharing power and influence.

Chapter Five – Unplugging

Are you unfocused or *too* focused? Chapter Five highlights the difficulty you probably have shifting between two types of attention: selective attention and open awareness. Plugging your attention into one focused activity requires unplugging your attention from another. This shift is difficult for your brain and represents the common problem of attention management. Your brain can be *too* focused, as it is when lost in a daydream, or brainlocked in an activity that is stimulating or urgent, but unimportant. Chapter Five presents strategies for shifting your attention. It addresses habitual mindlessness, time-wasters, destructive indulgences, and excuses.

Chapter Six – Creating

Your brain may be wired for creativity, but the neurological differences will not guarantee realizing your creative potential. I challenge a belief that you might hold: that you are not creative. Because you have difficulty activating and sustaining your effort, you may doubt your potential for creating. You may not have fully experienced the rewards of sustained effort. Chapter Six highlights how habitual, negative self-talk ("You're not creative... you're a fraud...you never finish anything!") inhibits creativity. It cites evidence of exceptional potential in the brains of individuals with ADHD and encourages experimentation.

Chapter Seven – ADHD is Funny. . . And It's Not

Jokes about ADHD abound. Many of them are harmless and even repeated by individuals with the disorder. But some are demeaning and offensive. You may laugh at yourself and joke with other like-minded individuals and family members. But some jokes imply a lack of intelligence or common sense. Chapter Seven relates your past experiences to current experiences of feeling misunderstood and devalued. In your past, you may have experienced victimization by bullies, alienation from peers, and punishment by parents and teachers. Jokes can trigger emotional memories associated with rejection. This chapter addresses how to relate to that history so it does not lend to rejecting yourself.

Chapter Eight – Success Stories

Chapter Eight highlights extraordinary successes of ordinary individuals like you. These particular adults with ADHD are people I know personally. Other books on ADHD typically identify successful, well-known individuals in history whose biographies suggest that they might have had the disorder—like Thomas Edison, Albert Einstein, and Winston Churchill. In this book, I describe the experiences of individuals who overachieved relative to the expectations of their families, peers, and teachers. These examples provide inspiring models.

Chapter Nine – The Color of Life: Living Skillfully with Your Emotions

Emotion regulation is an understated challenge for many individuals with ADHD. Chapter Nine was inspired by recent discoveries about neuroplasticity and the benefits of meditation. The brain concurrently perceives an external world and its own internal activity. The internal activity includes thoughts and emotions, imagined future events, and anticipated feelings (e.g., fearing the feeling of fear). We can easily confuse thoughts about experience with actual experience. The practice of observing external events (activity *outside* the brain) and internal events (activity *of* the brain) are themes of Chapter Nine. It illustrates the brain's remarkable capacity to change itself and how that capacity can serve you.

Chapter Ten – A Labor of Love: Using the Tools in Your Toolbox

Chapter Ten describes the tools for living well with ADHD and encourages you to get started using them. Its aim is to move you beyond attention to obstacles, negative thinking, and even the tools themselves—toward possibilities and opportunities instead.

It prescribes effort and practice. Its message is an alternative to *changing your brain to change your life*, focusing instead on *accepting your brain to skillfully manage your life* (which will change your brain). It assumes that your Zen mind is not to be left on the cushion, but to be used as a tool for living well in your daily life. This chapter includes a perspective on medicine as a tool.

Appendix—Starting and Leading an ADHD Support Group

I founded ADDNashville in 2005. This support group for adults has more than one hundred current members registered on its Yahoo Groups site, which includes only those participants who signed up for automatic email reminders of meetings. The appendix addresses both the mistakes and successes I have encountered along the way, as ADDNashville evolved. It includes tips for starting a support group, guidelines for participation, and suggestions for group leaders. It highlights some insights and strategies that participants have offered.

I wrote this book to help you embrace your life. It is the only life you will have. You can't come back and do it over once it is over. I want to help you to live a life that you value. I want you to discover your gifts and be creative, know how to connect more fully with others, experience the joy of activating and sustaining effort, pursue excellence, live with passion, and attain your life goals.

Both of my parents passed on before I began writing this book. They saw me start many projects that I never finished, a common experience among those of us who grew up with ADHD. They wouldn't buy me a set of drums because they believed that would be just one more thing I would start and not finish. I don't blame them. In my life, I have started and stopped piano lessons, guitar lessons, songwriting, essay and short story writing, novel writing, photography, jobs, books I was reading, and gardens I was growing.

And now, I have finished something I started. I hope reading this book is as valuable to you as writing it has been for me.

Chapter One

Who You Are and Who You Are Not

Do you ever ask yourself, "Who am I?" Many people ask that question throughout their adult lives. As a person with ADHD, the answer may be especially elusive...because you've probably been branded and mislabeled your entire life.

Have any of the following painful labels ever been ascribed to you?

- You are unmotivated.

- You are unwilling to apply yourself.

- You don't try hard enough.

- You are uninterested in things.

- You are unconcerned about others.

- You are unable to focus.

In this chapter we will examine some truths that begin with two especially important ones:

You are not your ADHD symptoms. And you are not what teachers and parents said you are.

You are not your symptoms of ADHD, nor the habits you may have developed because of them. If you have ADHD, you probably have trouble starting tasks that are not urgent, novel, or personally stimulating. And once you start, you may interrupt yourself often and have to start again and again. It's hard enough to start just once!

If you're like me, you may jump tracks often, abandoning many unfinished tasks. I read a lot and finish about half the books I begin. If I'm not hooked after a few chapters, I will stop and then start another book. Many of the books on my shelf still have bookmarks in them, revealing where I stopped reading. Some have multiple bookmarks because I skip a lot.

You probably misplace items often, have trouble estimating and tracking time, and drift in and out of attentiveness when reading or listening to lectures. You likely have trouble organizing, you tend to clutter your desk, and you have an aversion to tedious detail work unless it is related to some passionate interest. You feel restless or bored easily. You may interrupt others, and you may have trouble waiting in lines or at traffic stops. You probably wait until close to a deadline before starting time-sensitive tasks, such as writing a term paper, paying a bill, studying for an exam, or preparing a presentation. Procrastination creates urgency, and urgency activates your ADHD brain. It "treats" ADHD, in a manner of speaking, and a writing assignment is not urgent until the night before it is due. Pressed against the deadline, you focus and get it done, even though this habitual pattern doesn't allow sufficient time to do your best.

You may often arrive late for appointments because you were occupied with something before departing. You probably have difficulty estimating and tracking time. And you may have a history of trouble with relationships. You don't always listen attentively. For example, your partner may begin telling you about a mutual friend's serious accident while you are driving past a new park that you want her to see. You hear her talking, but your mind is already on the park. If you don't point it out right away, the opportunity to show her the park will have passed. After interrupting to show her the park, you return your attention to *her* and she no longer wants to talk to you. You realize too late what you have done. You are sincerely shocked and saddened at the news that your wife communicated, once you actually process it. But to her, you appear insensitive, and the evidence supports her perception.

These are common effects of having an ADHD brain. An under-performing attention manager can cause significant life problems.

ADHD is defined by more than the features. To get an accurate diagnosis, other plausible explanations for the features must be ruled out. The symptoms have to affect your functioning significantly and in more than one environment. And the symptoms must have been present early in life, before adulthood.

What, exactly, is the anatomy of an ADHD brain? How is it different from the typical brain? Science has offered different explanations. Some studies have shown less activity and less volume in certain areas of the ADHD brain—as much as 14 percent less volume in the anterior cingulate cortex and 8.3 percent in the frontal lobe area, according to one Harvard study. Overall, there is widespread evidence of differences in volume and activity in the ADHD brain, but it has been difficult to pin down consistent differences in specific regions.[1] That three-pound sponge—with its 86 billion cells and trillions of connections—is a complex organ. There is clear evidence also of differences in brain chemistry. We know that boosting the release of dopamine enhances attention and alertness. Research at Vanderbilt University pointed to differences in the genetic transporter of dopamine in the ADHD brain.

I am not a researcher; I prefer to read the research and let the researchers write about it. Exploring the science of ADHD can be a validating experience, however, and a reminder that this condition is real. In addition to reading the science that explains the disorder, one should read the science about non-medical remedies. We know that a healthy diet, sufficient sleep, and regular exercise are good for anyone's brain. And there is a growing body of knowledge about the positive effects of meditation on the brain, including positive effects on the ADHD brain in particular. I traded my medication for meditation because nothing has helped me more. Still, I am a proponent of medication for those who can benefit without side effects. I have seen medicine change lives and save marriages.

You and your doctor need to determine if medication is right for you. Most people benefit from it. But to illustrate just one kind of problem one might encounter with medicine, let me share a true story with you.

One of the last times I took Adderall, I was proud at the end of the day that I was finishing my paperwork seamlessly. I was laser-focused until a phone call jolted me out of my "selective attention." It was after six o'clock when I suddenly realized I had left my dog at a veterinary clinic just walking distance from my office. They closed at five-thirty. I rushed out of my building to drive the short distance there and see if someone might still be at the clinic. But I could not find my car in the office parking lot. Then I remembered having left it to be serviced at Firestone that morning, right across from the animal hospital. Firestone closed at six. I felt horrible, having abandoned my dog and misplaced my car. I called my wife and told her what happened.

"I'm walking to Local Taco," I said. "I'm going to have a margarita and dinner, and when I'm done I will call you to come and get me."

So, for me, a side effect of medication trumped the benefits. It locked me into a focused state too much. But for many adults with ADHD, perhaps most, medication makes a positive difference. Trust your own experience. There is no better expert on your experience than you.

So, let's return to the all-important question: Who are you?

• You are *not* who your parents may have told you you are.

• You are *not* what your teachers may have told you you are.

• You are *not* the labels people may have placed on you for much of your life.

• You are *not* your ADHD symptoms.

That's *not* who you are.

As a psychotherapist specializing in attention disorders, I have observed ADHD for many years and heard many stories. I remember my meeting with the first adult I ever diagnosed with ADHD. She told me that when she was growing up, her father often said to her, "If your brain was in a bird, it would fly backward." And my own parents told me, "You would lose your head if it wasn't attached."

If "who you are" has been overly influenced by what others have said about you—by the labels they have thrown on you—then you may be carrying, within yourself, negative portrayals from others who didn't know better. You may be carrying inaccurate notions about yourself, taken in before you knew you had ADHD, or before you understood what it means…and what it *doesn't* mean.

It is very important that you fully understand this:

You don't have a *deficit* of attention.

In fact, you probably have a surplus. The real problem is that, if you have ADHD, your *attention manager* goes to sleep on the job. It takes too many breaks. This may be forcing you to attempt the impossible, to attend to too many things at once. You don't know where to start. Your efforts are interrupted by other tasks competing for your attention. You often miss out on the natural rewards of completing a task. You are always behind.

You don't lack the ability to focus; your ability is just inconsistent. Think about it. You can be as focused as anyone in activity that is personally stimulating or novel. But you have great difficulty sustaining your attention and effort when you are under-stimulated.

Following are three additional, vitally important points for you to understand:

You are *not* your thoughts.

You are *not* an expert on your spouse's intentions.

You *are* someone meant to create.

Let's look at these points, one at a time:

You are not your thoughts. Direct experience does not require a narrative in thought. You can observe your experience without applying language to what you are observing. It is true that mental activity is a direct experience, but you are not the thought itself. You are *someone who can think.*

And remember this: Your thought can be an incorrect assumption, or a distortion of some objective truth. For example, you might be angry about not being invited to a friend's wedding, only to learn later that she sent your invitation to the wrong address. At first, you had the *thought* that you were excluded, but you were not. In other words, you were not your thought.

A larger lesson to take from this is: Suspending certainty can be healthy. "Always keep a don't-know mind," Zen Master Seung Sahn often told his students. "Our don't-know mind can do anything." [2]

You are not an expert on your spouse's intentions. If you are not your thoughts, then assumptions about your partner's intentions are just your thoughts. They are not the same as her intentions. Only she knows her intentions. When she is angry, you can get closer to the truth of her experience by being curious instead of angry that she is angry. Asking her to tell you more will disarm her. Being defensive, on the other hand, will communicate to her that your feelings are more important than her complaint. Those of us with ADHD tend to get defensive easily because many of us have a history of being misunderstood.

Having ADHD, you can get lost in the limited sphere of your thoughts all too easily and confuse them with absolute truth. Experiencing thoughts as just thoughts can help you to be more patient and understanding in relation to others. A thought can only be an imperfect reflection of some truth, but not the truth itself.

You are someone meant to create. I believe you were born to create. You may not buy it because it doesn't fit what you were told about yourself. But I think all humans are meant to create. Why else are you here? It hurts me to hear so many people say that there is not one creative bone in their body. I don't believe it. Having ADHD, you may, in fact, have a creativity *advantage*, but only if you make an effort to use your creative potential.

Here's something to try, even if you don't believe you're creative: Pretend you are creative for a few months and see what happens. When you are imaginative and hyper-focused on some endeavor, you are in the creative zone. You can get so lost in the activity that you hardly know anyone is around, and you have no idea what time it is. You may even forget to eat when engaged in your passion. But to sustain creative endeavors and actually produce, you will have to learn how to sustain a steady effort, to run marathons instead of sprints. You will need to develop the skill of shifting your awareness—between a focused and an open state.

You will need to know how to activate, sustain your effort, and put on the brakes. I will go into more detail about getting started and sustaining effort in the next chapter.

Don't believe those who say that you can't focus. That's just a misperception that others may have had about you. It is more accurate to say that you have difficulty *managing* your attention, shifting your focus from one kind of activity to another and sustaining your effort. You get overwhelmed when you have to prioritize. But when you are focused, you are focused—and you know it.

I like being around ADHD brains. I have had the privilege of meeting many sensitive, creative, and uncensored men and women who see things that others miss. I have seen it time and again in my psychotherapy practice and in my support group. In the support group, insightful observations are often framed as no one but an adult with ADHD would frame them.

As someone with ADHD, you may have an aversion to the tedium of details, but you get the big picture. No respectful professional would want to overhaul your ADHD brain. The job of a professional is to help you learn to live well with the brain you have.

A professional should be helping you to do the following things:

- accept your differences as differences rather than deficits
- know your strengths as well as your challenges
- correct inaccurate notions you carry about yourself
- practice ways of cultivating mindful awareness
- be gentle with yourself and drop the judgment
- stop blaming others…and yourself
- borrow from the detail-oriented brains of others and contribute from your visionary brain in exchange
- use technology and tools as extensions of your brain
- unlock your creative potential

Professionals experienced in treating ADHD can help you stop wishing your brain was wired a different way and live well with the brain you were given. I agree with Julia Cameron (*The Artist's Way*), Natalie Goldberg (*Writing Down the Bones*), and Brenda Ueland (*If You Want to Write*), all of whom suggest that we are born to create, but then we are taught to censor ourselves. Their books help individuals recover their natural creativity. Too often, individuals with ADHD have been taught not to create. We do things our way and get tagged as defiant. Maybe we should defy the tag!

"There are so many colors in the rainbow."

Years ago, I saw Harry Chapin perform at the Greek Theater in Hollywood. He introduced a song he had recorded on his album, *Living Room Suite*. "Flowers are Red" was inspired, he said, by the experience of a neighbor's son who had just started kindergarten. The child had gone off happily to school and returned that afternoon with his spirit crushed. The song is about a teacher's assault on a child's creative nature. The teacher was correcting the student on his first day of school for using all the colors in his crayon box to color flowers. In his two-part chorus, Chapin created a dialogue between the teacher and the student. The teacher told her new student that flowers are red and leaves are green, and he needed to use only those colors. She called him "sassy" when he resisted. In the song, Chapin has the child replying, "There are so many colors in the rainbow, so many colors in the morning sun, so many colors in the flowers, and I see every one."

The teacher punished the child for not doing what he was told. He became lonely and scared when the teacher made him stand in a corner of the classroom. So, he complied and told her what she wanted to hear, that flowers are red and leaves are green. The next year, the child and his family moved to another town where the boy went to a new school. His new teacher was smiling as she said, "Painting should be fun." She instructed her students to use all the colors. But her new student continued to paint flowers "in neat rows of green and red." The teacher asked him why. Having learned a harsh lesson from his former teacher, he replied, "There's no need to see flowers any other way than the way they always have been seen." Chapin sang this last line at a much slower tempo to emphasize the sad lesson learned.

Was this young boy what his teacher told him he was? At the Greek Theatre that night, Chapin chose to end the song differently from his studio recording of it. Pausing briefly after singing the child's sad reply to his new smiling teacher, he said it would have been nice if this story had ended another way, and he began singing the uplifting second part of the chorus in the original tempo: "There are so many colors in the rainbow, so many colors in the morning sun, so many colors in the flowers and I see every one."[3]

KEY POINTS TO PONDER:

- As a person with ADHD, you are not who others have said you are. The negative labels people may have thrown on you are not true.

- You are not the same as your ADHD symptoms.

- You probably have a *surplus* of attention, rather than a deficit. You simply may have difficulty managing your attention.

- Your ADHD brain can be a wonderful gift, allowing you to be uniquely observant and creative.

QUESTIONS FOR REFLECTION:

- What negative things have people said about you because of your ADHD? Did those things change the way you have thought about yourself?

- What does the following mean to you personally? *You are not your ADHD symptoms.*

- Regarding your ADHD symptoms, what has been your experience with meditation versus medication?

- In what ways does your ADHD brain give you unique insight and creativity?

Chapter Two

Wash One Dish:
How to Activate Attention and Sustain Effort

Do you, or do other people, think you are lazy? I suppose you could be, but how would you know? And what does it mean anyway? The concept of laziness may describe something, but it doesn't explain anything. I never met anyone who aspired to be incompetent, or wished to achieve nothing. The concept suggests a character flaw. If you buy the suggestion that you are a lazy person, you may find it especially hard to start a task. But suppose you are not lazy, and that any lack of motivation is due to this inaccurate notion about your character and worth. I want you to entertain a different theory about yourself—that you simply have a brain difference that makes it difficult for you to activate your attention. Remember in the previous chapter how the manager in your brain goes to sleep on the job? There is more to activating than meets the eye. Getting started on most tasks is a complex neurological sequence of activity, requiring coordination of various regions of the brain.

For example, when you write a paper, your brain has to:

- use its long-term memory to access a knowledge base
- use its short-term memory to temporarily park information
- focus your eyes for reading
- track the lines on the page when reading
- read and process printed material
- synthesize and summarize information
- create an outline for thoughts
- convert thoughts into sentences
- organize sentences into a meaningful order
- navigate the mechanics of writing or typing

Just as a symphony conductor is responsible for coordinating the activities of musicians to perform complex compositions, the brain's executive command center coordinates the activities of various parts of the brain that perform the complex task of writing. But the "symphony" conductor in the ADHD brain is not consistently alert and on the job.

In this chapter we are going to explore:

- why it is hard to start certain kinds of tasks
- why you have trouble finishing the task at hand before starting another
- what you can do to activate your attention and sustain your effort

Activating

Difficulty activating may be the biggest, most understated problem for adults with ADHD. Hearing those words at an ADD conference long ago liberated me from years of harsh self-criticism. To say that someone is not motivated is not accurate. All human behavior, by definition, is motivated. The question should be why someone is more motivated to engage in one activity over another. Why would a student be more motivated to surf the Internet than to begin a reading assignment?

To understand why the procrastinator is not starting, it is important to examine what he or she is doing instead. I have asked many individuals with ADHD what they are saying to themselves when failing to start. Adolescents who avoid starting homework consistently give the same answer: "I have time...I'll do it later." It is an interesting answer considering that they don't estimate or track time well. They can't conceptualize how long their work is going to take. What they mean is that they have time to do what they'd rather do and save just enough time to squeeze in their homework. They seldom *allow* enough time, and they often forget anyway. They make two erroneous assumptions:

- **They know how much time the assignment will take.**
- **They will remember to do it.**

11

I'm amazed at how many adolescents with ADHD willingly change their patterns and start homework earlier once they grasp how it serves their interest. If they start their work right away, upon arrival from school, they won't have to stop a preferred activity in order to start a dreaded task. Their video game won't be interrupted by a frustrated parent who wants them to stop the fun and start the homework. And they can complete their work more quickly if they begin doing it while medicine is still in effect. Their parents will be more supportive of their preferred activities if work is completed first. Their parents might even get off their backs!

You probably create a lot of your own stress with your inner dialogue. Your self-talk may often be harsh and demanding: "I need to quit putting it off...I don't know why I keep procrastinating... I'm just lazy...I feel like a loser." Self-talk can be unreasonable and self-defeating: "It's going to take too much time...I don't have enough time." Saying those words won't help. Self-criticism is just more cognitive activity on top of the excessive cognitive activity that is typical of individuals with ADHD. Furthermore, your defiant streak may be as strong as your self-criticism. Your harsh internal voices battle one another. The commander is rebuffed by the rebel: "Just get off your butt and start! You can't make me!"

Even when you realize that the harsh self-criticism only does harm, you become critical about your tendency to be self-critical. "Oh, there I go again. I hate that I do that!" The key to ending this cycle is simply to observe without judgment. You might say to yourself, "There's that critical judge." I prefer to abbreviate the observation with just the two simple words: *"There's that."* It is a way of saying, "There is that tendency popping up again," without any judgment about the tendency. What is wrong with a tendency anyway? Framing the self-criticism as a tendency takes its power away. Whereas, judgment catapults you back into a stream of thinking, and excessive thinking is much of the problem. What could be more distracting than a stream of superfluous chatter running through your brain?

So, what activities are competing for your attention, drawing you away from the task at hand? Individuals with ADHD tend to be drawn like a magnet to novelty, urgency, and passionate interests, and away from activities that are routine, non-urgent, and uninteresting. The former appear to create a surge of neurochemical action in the brain, and dopamine is one of those brain-activating chemicals. It is a chemical that most ADHD medicines target, and one that is essential to focusing, organizing tasks, starting, and sustaining effort. To illustrate how ADHD affects our behavior, answer this question: Why do you suppose you are suddenly able to focus your attention and sustain your effort when pressed against a deadline? You guessed it. You created urgency after postponing starting and, eventually, the neurochemical boost from urgency allowed you to start and focus. So, you can see how procrastinating can easily become a habit of the mind, as it is reinforced by the eventual "urgency effect."

Meeting a new client is more novel and more stimulating than writing progress notes. Making a sale is more urgent than completing an expense report. Video games are all three. Every action in a video game is urgent, each moment is novel, and the activity is stimulating. It is no wonder that 14-year-olds with ADHD don't respond well to parents who interrupt them with, "Stop playing that game now and start your homework!" Or, "Get off the phone now and do your chores!" Unaware of an undiagnosed ADHD, many parents bring their kids to therapy for "anger problems." The abrupt interruption of their selective attention just feels unbearable to them. There is no deficit of attention when someone with ADHD is brainlocked in a stimulating task. The same brain that can't seem to start and sustain attention to an academic task cannot withdraw from the more personally stimulating and urgent activity. In truth, the problem is not so much attention *deficit* as it is attention *inconsistency*. Attention management disorder would be a better name for this neurological difference.

13

The parent who is sensitive to the nature of the ADHD will give some notice to their adolescent: "Look at the clock now and be aware that you will need to stop soon." And then she will suggest an interim activity that allows open awareness and prevents a hyperfocused state. She may suggest a snack or physical activity before beginning homework, activities that don't require focused attention, making it easier to shift from open awareness into focusing on homework. Shifting from focusing on a game to focusing on homework is difficult. Think about it. It's like going to happy hour before going to work! Competing with dopamine-boosting activities is no less challenging for adults with ADHD. Meeting the challenge requires intentional effort and creative strategies.

The notion of not having enough time is a delusion. We all have the same amount of time. The problems have less to do with amount of time than inability to prioritize. Prioritizing is essential to activating. Experts say that individuals with ADHD prioritize horizontally rather than vertically. That is to say, all tasks have equal priority. But that only means that you simply don't prioritize, except perhaps by novelty, urgency, and personal passion. Otherwise, you just don't know where to start if no one task is more or less important than another.

You need to stop not starting.

The term "procrastination" is part of the problem here. I often ask my clients, "What does it mean to stop procrastinating?" They reply, "It means being unable to start."

"So, what do you mean?" I ask. "Are you saying that you need to stop not starting? What does it mean to stop not starting?"

They usually laugh at the absurdity of their habitual thought. It is more direct and meaningful to substitute the word "activate" for stopping procrastination. *Strategies* for activating point you in some direction, unlike *thoughts* about failing to start. Such thoughts don't serve any purpose. Saying that you need to stop procrastinating, or that you ought to start this task now, is not the same as actually starting. It is only chatter that will distract and obstruct you.

I have attended a number of three-day meditation retreats over the past two decades. In the beginning I noticed that the silent work period, following the silent lunch, was much more pleasant than sitting on a cushion and meditating for hours. I experienced more pleasure in activity than inactivity. Standing at the kitchen sink and washing dishes was peaceful. And it was the same task that I hated at home. Why was that? The purpose of practicing meditation, I learned, was not to get away from life, but to embrace the activity of life. I learned what it meant to engage in an activity with mindful attention to what I'm doing. At the retreat I was simply moving *toward* the activity of washing dishes rather than *away* from it. At home, I tended to avoid it. When I learned to move toward the task willingly, washing dishes was not a problem. The *task* had never been my problem; the only problem was my *habitual thought.* My internal voice had been pushing back against a task that, in reality, is simple. The chatter was the only thing making it aversive. Like painting a room black and then complaining of darkness, I had been painting the task in a dark color.

I recall having joked to my wife years ago, after hosting a social event at our house, that I would rather burn down the kitchen than wash all those dishes. There was a time when I would turn on the TV or radio, as if the task required some kind of distraction to prevent boredom. I would then become obsessive about which channel to watch, or whether to listen to the radio or to recorded music, or to the news. Sometimes I would even alternate among the different forms of stimulation, wasting precious time trying not to be bored. It's no wonder I hated the task.

Boredom is largely delusion anyway, a mistaken notion that we cannot tolerate restless feelings. It is only true if you believe it. If you quit bothering yourself about restless feelings that rise within you, and you learn to tolerate them instead, then what is boredom?

One evening, after a birthday party at my house, my wife said she would wash the dishes the next morning. "I have to get off my feet because my arthritis is bothering me," she said. "It's your birthday. Just leave them for me to wash in the morning."

When she left the kitchen, I turned toward the mounds of dishes. I caught myself starting to "awfulize" about the magnitude of the task and interrupted the rising thoughts with one simple action: *I washed one dish.* I washed it unhurriedly, giving full attention to what I was doing, and without committing to wash any more in that moment. I was not "cleaning the kitchen," but just washing one dish. It was liberating and easy to repeat the same activity. It was late and the house was quiet. There were no distractions. I continued to pick up just one dish and wash it without any noisy chatter in my head, and with my full attention.

Rather than wishing to get out of the task, I got into it. Thoughts associated with getting out of it began to vanish. Choosing to focus only on the dish, I had nothing else in the world to worry about. I had no problems to solve in that time, just a simple activity that I could embrace with undivided attention. In time, washing dishes became as peaceful at home as it was at the meditation retreats. It became, in fact, a way of practicing mindfulness at home. My primary goal was no longer to have a clean kitchen, but to have a clear mind. The clean kitchen was a bonus.

Tasks with multiple steps might seem overwhelming to you. You see the whole more clearly than the parts. You don't easily conceptualize one step as if it were all you had to do. It is hard to start when you cannot imagine finishing.

What if you just started without undue attention to finishing, and without bemoaning how long the task will take? Engaging in just one manageable part of a task without the distraction of thoughts, especially negative thoughts, is peaceful. Peace comes from being mindfully present right where you are, in one place and at one moment in time, not trying to escape into a supposed better place or time. It is the peace that comes from silencing the "awfulizing" voice and substituting action for thought. To substitute an action for a thought is to shut up and wash one dish, to quiet your mind by activating, by starting the task. Once you have turned that corner and interrupted the chatter with action, the peace will follow immediately. You may have to take a leap of faith here in order to learn better from your own direct experience than from my words!

While washing one dish is manageable, you may still begin to "awfulize" again when you get to the pots and pans. Your mental noise can rise endlessly, but you can return to silence any time by substituting action for thought—i.e., by activating. Of course, pots and pans are much nastier than plates and glasses (here is the chatter again!). Still, you can wash one pot. It is no different. You can abandon negative thoughts the moment they arise, and then act. Being liberated from the constant wish to be finished, unencumbered from trying to escape the present, you will experience the peace of activating. If you want to get out of it, get into it.

Sustaining Your Effort

- Do you feel overwhelmed by competing obligations, by too much on your plate?

- Do you find yourself starting many tasks and finishing few of them?

- Do you have as much trouble pulling your attention out of a preferred activity as you do shifting into a dreaded one?

Sustaining effort is another common problem for adults with ADHD. You may start one task and then get drawn to another before completing the first. Repeatedly returning to the first task means having to activate again and again. Thus, you create more activation problems with your approach to tasks. You work so hard and so inefficiently. You spin in circles.

One strategy for sustaining effort is creating an environment exclusively for one particular activity, like a designated place and a particular block of time. Behavioral psychologists call it "stimulus control." When you enter into that environment—that place and that time—you are more likely to engage in the intended activity because competing activity is minimized. For example, when you enter a church or a meditation center, you don't even think of answering a phone, getting a snack, chatting with someone next to you, or getting up and down from your seat. You engage in the activity of worship or meditation.

Early in college, I made average grades until I began doing all my work in the library rather than in my apartment. The apartment had a television, loud music, loud roommates, and beer. The library had none of those things. When I sat down at a study carrel, I studied. There was no food there, my friends were not there, there was no music (long before iPods and iPads), and I was motivated to get out of there, which helped me to start and keep working. I was seamless in completing my work and better able to keep it organized. All I did was change my environment, which was much easier than changing my brain. I felt I had more time to enjoy my life than when I was "trying" to study in the apartment.

Most of us don't have a sanctuary at home, a space we can reserve for just one kind of task, and so we may have to improvise. You may have a card table that is seldom used, or a dining room table that only gets used for special occasions. You can use them for stimulus control. If there are too many distractions in your office, especially if you work in a cubicle, maybe you can find a conference room that is not used frequently. When you enter into that chosen space and that protected block of time, you are increasing your chance of activating and sustaining your effort. Sustaining this stimulus control routine may be challenging at first, but even adults with ADHD can form new habits. All you have to do is keep repeating the routine and experiencing the inherent rewards. That is how habits are formed. And here is good news for you: Habits and memory are not the same. Parts of the brain involved in developing and storing habits are not the same as the parts that manage memory. You can have a poor working memory and still cultivate new habits that support activating and sustaining your effort.

**Give up trying to act like
those who do not have ADHD.**

Trying to become an organized person, and criticizing yourself for failing to be one, is a prescription for failure. You don't have to be an organized student to have a well-organized binder, a digital reminder, or a user-friendly word processing program. You don't have to become an organized person to do your work in your "sanctuary" instead of a noisy environment.

You should give up trying to be like those who do not have ADHD. I tell my clients, "If you have ADHD, then act like it! You are in the five percent club. Stop trying to be like the other ninety-five percent." The minority does not have to be like the majority. Accepting your differences allows you to define your challenges accurately and stop wishing to be some other way. Wishing to be some other way causes you to suffer. You have suffered enough!

When you define your challenges accurately, you will discover more successful strategies. Kicking yourself assumes that the problem is of a motivational nature, and it won't work. Motivation is not the problem, although it can become a problem if you continue to criticize yourself, or engage in other self-defeating behavior. Helplessness is unhelpful!

Rather than try harder, *try another way.* I have had clients tell me that they need to try harder to remember. I often reply, "Show me what it looks like to try hard to remember something." They usually laugh at this nonsense and feel relief from years of such habitual thinking. Well-meaning parents tell their ADHD teens to try harder to focus, try harder to remember to bring your text books home, try harder to start working, try to go to sleep. (Trying to go to sleep will keep you awake!)

Try another strategy! Be creative! Just don't give up!

While you will not likely become your ideal of an organized person, you can create an environment that makes sustained attention and effort easy. The strategy of stimulus control can be useful for the gifted salesperson who doesn't complete required paperwork in a timely manner. You can bring the expense report forms and credit card receipts to the table without giving too much thought to completing the task—committing instead just to start. You can engage mindfully in one step as if it is all you have to do. You can activate by just sorting the expense reports and receipts by date (i.e., you can *wash one dish*). After sorting the paper, you will more easily see the next step and commit only to washing that next dish, the one that is in your hand. You don't have to keep looking beyond the task at hand and getting overwhelmed.

Manageable tasks can seem insurmountable because your big-picture brain doesn't easily break a job down into doable steps. An aspiring writer with ADHD told a friend that he could not imagine writing a 250-page book, until the friend asked him if he could write five pages a week. Without pause, he said he could easily write five pages a week. He completed a manuscript within one year.

The only *activity* in boredom is the activity of repeating the thought, "This is boring."

A friend once told me, as he was beginning a meditation practice, that he could meditate for no more than five minutes before he had to get up and pace. After pacing, he could sit for five more minutes. What he was suggesting was simply not true, and I told him so. He believed that he could not tolerate restless feelings. I suggested that when that notion arose during his meditation, he should treat it like any other thought. I told him just to sit through it without bothering himself about restlessness. He began to practice dropping his story line of not being able to tolerate restless feelings. He tolerated them, not by convincing himself, but by practicing tolerating them.

You may think that redundant paperwork and household chores are boring, but coloring those tasks as such is unhelpful. Judging necessary tasks as good or bad, interesting or boring, easy or difficult, will only obstruct you from embracing them. The notion of getting the dishes out of the way in order to get to real life, like surfing the Internet or watching television, is the ultimate delusion. Eating and cleaning up afterward are as real as life gets! Such tasks have been central to life from the beginning.

To take a single step into any task at hand, rather than stepping away from it, is to activate. Continuing to engage mindfully in the activity, without excessive focus on the finish line, will help you sustain an easy pace and complete the task. By definition, there is no aversion when moving toward an activity. And when you cross the finish line, you get to experience the inherent reward of a job completed...and the gratitude of others who benefit.

You don't have to assign negative value to necessary tasks. Substituting action for thought will tame the beast of excessive thought and make your goals attainable. So stop saying, "It is boring." The only real *activity* that represents the concept of boredom is repeating the thought *This is boring!*

That leads us to what may be the best treatment for ADHD. What could be more stimulating—hence easy to start and sustain—than activity that naturally fuels you? If you have a passion for a certain activity, you should make time for it. Don't wait for some *other* time. That time may never come. Protect time for your passion and for activities that are in line with your values. At least begin. If the activities are stimulating beyond startup, or if they represent adventures into new frontiers, then you are likely to sustain your effort.

I have known several individuals with ADHD who worked passionately while starting up their businesses and then became uninspired with the challenges of operating them. The businesses failed. Running them was unlike starting them. A client once asked me why she could never seem to do her job as well as her fellow teachers. She disliked the job. She could not divide her attention in the many ways required of teachers. She was disorganized. She had been laid off from teaching jobs more than once. I responded awkwardly, asking, "Why should you do well what you so dislike?" (I never talk like that; I don't even read Shakespeare!) She understood and, soon after, she gave up teaching and pursued another graduate degree. She became a successful speech pathologist, working with just one client at a time and loving it.

I have known others who could hardly say no to any new and interesting project that came along, no matter how busy they were. They had no problem activating. They had the opposite problem— no brakes on chasing the new, urgent opportunity. As new opportunities came, the least urgent priorities would keep getting pushed to the bottom of the list and eventually neglected. New projects would command the most attention. In some cases, they neglected needs of their families because those needs were not novel, and often not urgent (until the threat of divorce made them so). If you are hyperactive and impulsive, you should practice pausing before saying yes to something new, and be ready to say "no" as your default response. Being better prepared to decline a request will allow you time to give more thoughtful consideration to existing obligations and priorities.

Anyone can wash one dish. Through practice, you can learn to activate and sustain your attention and effort. You won't get there just by thinking differently. Mindful presence is something you must cultivate through practice in your daily life. John Dewey once said that the best learning experience in the long run is to be so fully present in each moment that you can take from that moment all that it has to offer. To sacrifice the present for a supposed future is something other than living in real time—awake in each moment—where life happens.

Through practice, you can learn how to:

- turn the corner on starting
- maintain a steady pace of effort
- finish what you begin

KEY POINTS TO PONDER:

- It is simply a brain difference that makes it hard for you to activate.

- You have no less time than others. But if no task is more or less important than another, you have trouble knowing where to start.

- You often feel overwhelmed because you don't easily conceptualize one step as if it is all you have to do.

- Having a designated place and time for certain activities increases your chance of starting promptly and sustaining your effort.

- You should give up trying to act as if you are no different from those who do not have ADHD.

- Substitute "Try another way" for "Try harder."

- To continue without undue concern for finishing helps you to sustain effort…and finish.

QUESTIONS FOR REFLECTION:

- What harsh and demanding things do you say to yourself when you're having trouble starting?

- What harm does it do to speak harshly to yourself when trying to get motivated to begin?

- Why do you feel like you have less time than others to get things done? What can you do about this?

- What is the connection between washing a single dish and getting started on a task?

- What does it mean to be mindfully present?

Chapter Three

Attentive Listening and Mindful Speaking

Attentive Listening

When someone smiles at you, you may feel a warm sensation in your body, and you are likely to smile back. What is that? No one laid a hand on you, and yet that brief visual input stimulated a physical change in you. The smile "touched" you. Humans are connected to one another by brains that function collectively. Like a satellite receiver, your amazing brain can pick up subtle signals of nonverbal communication. Its reception of the smile immediately took on meaning that connected you to that person. The experience involved your body, your language and thoughts, your culture, your personal history, and your family's history. It meant something because:

- You have brain cells (mirror neurons) dedicated to "reading" the expressions and posture of others.

- You attach *meaning* to nonverbal signals through language and thought.

- The *observing* and *interpreting* regions of your brain interact with the feeling regions.

- Your culture *makes meaning* of the feeling based on shared history.

- The *collective experience* of your family and your ancestors has created a *file* of similar experiences.

- Your *personal history* has its own file of experiences.

We are more than isolated individuals. We are also body parts—parts of a social body. We have survived as a species because of it. Listening and speaking are your means of connecting with others. If you are not listening with your full attention, the speaker will experience an absence of connection with you. If your speech is too vague or excessive, the listener will not have a chance to connect.

In this chapter we will explore:

• the nature of your inattention when listening

• your difficulty conveying thoughts clearly when speaking

• what you can do about these challenges

Just as your attentiveness is variable, your mindfulness of others may be inconsistent. You can get so lost in your own thoughts while interacting with someone, you lose awareness of your listener. At the moment this happens, you are unaware of the disconnect from them. That is why you might not understand your relationship partner when she tells you that she feels unimportant, neglected, or lonely. This is what one member of my ADHD support group called "unintentional narcissism." You can appear selfish when lost in your limited sphere of awareness.

Whatever your intentions, your behavior affects others, and you have to accept responsibility for your actions.

The individuals in my support group are among the most selfless people I know, and yet they experience episodes of unintentional narcissism. Does that mean they are *not* truly selfish because they don't intend to be, or they *are* selfish because actions speak louder than intentions? I once heard Lyle Lovett sing, "She wasn't good, but she had good intentions." Whatever your intentions, your behavior affects others, and you have to accept responsibility for your actions.

Negatively judging yourself does not help. It just adds more traffic to the busy streets of your mind. Any judgment of this elusive thing we call the self—whether negative or positive—is what one Japanese Zen master called "having a head on top of the head; you don't need the extra head."[4] It is pointless chatter. But judging your performance is different. So, stop asking, "Why can't I do this? What is wrong with me?" It is more useful to ask, "Can I do better? Can I find another way?"

You *can* do better! You can become a better listener. You can learn to connect more fully with others. It is beyond the scope of this book to explain how to cultivate mindfulness. Those books have already been written, including one specifically for adults with ADHD: Dr. Lidia Zylowska's *The Mindfulness Prescription for Adult ADHD*. Individuals with ADHD can learn mindfulness skills and learn how to direct their attention. Dr. Zalowska's book explains how to do this.[5] The practice can help you listen more fully with the intention of understanding.

You are capable of improving how you live with others through learning and practicing effective listening and mindful speaking. Because of how you are hardwired, you might not be as socially competent as you think you are, and you might be unaware of your unawareness. It's like failing to consider that you cannot find your eyeglasses because you can't see without them. Dr. Daniel Siegel, author of *The Mindful Brain*, says that "two of the essential elements of all mindful awareness practices appear to be an awareness of awareness itself and a focus of attention on intention."[6] The same regions of your brain responsible for attentiveness can be inattentive to the complexities and subtleties of social interaction.

Whatever the nature of your neurological differences, it is safe to say that your hardwiring contributes to your relationship challenges. You have biologically-based reasons for communication problems, including the problem of denying that you have those problems. If your relationship partner has a problem with you, and you feel you have no problem with her (except for her problem with you!), then you might erroneously conclude that the problem is simply hers. You will deny your own challenges because you don't see them.

Defensiveness is a relationship killer. When defensive, you insulate yourself from feedback. You take the speaker's presentation of a concern off the table and supplant it with your own. For example, she may have a valid criticism, but your feelings have you focusing on how she is talking to you, not what she is saying. Chances are, she is angry because of some effect of your

ADHD symptoms. And that is not a big problem when you recognize it and try to be helpful.

Despite your good intentions, and having received a lot of criticism in your life, you have probably been practicing defensiveness for years. So what can you do? You can practice something else—like tolerating your hurt feelings rather than mindlessly acting on them. Defensiveness is one way of trying not to have uncomfortable feelings. When you encourage your angry partner to say more about her experience, you may feel uncomfortable, but you will decrease her frustration or anger by listening respectfully. There is no need for your wife to keep holding the gun to your head when you invite her to say what she needs you to understand about why she is angry. If your partner has a problem with the relationship, then you have a problem with the relationship, and you have a responsibility as a partner to participate in resolving it.

What does it mean to listen attentively? Brenda Ueland wrote this:

> *, Now there are brilliant people who cannot listen much. They have no ingoing wires on their apparatus. They are entertaining, but exhausting, too.... Now before going to a party, I just tell myself to listen with affection to anyone who talks to me, to be in their shoes when they talk; to try to know them without my mind pressing against theirs, or arguing, or changing the subject.*[7]

When I played high school basketball, my coach taught me to "square up" to the basket. To square up meant to have both feet pointing toward the goal in order to have a good view and a balanced posture. Squaring up improved my shooting. I could see the goal and feel connected to it. If you square up when your relationship partner makes a bid for your attention, you will feel connected and she will notice. Turn toward your partner, make eye contact, and display a posture that says, "I am present and connected, ready to listen, and aware that what you have to say is important."

When your partner starts to tell you something about her day, you might appear uninterested. In fact, you might not experience a *feeling* of interest initially, especially if you have been hyperfocused on something else. So, you try to listen attentively, but you can't "see" enough of the picture to get the essence of the story. It isn't that you don't care, but the pieces of the puzzle are sparse at the beginning, and insufficient to seeing a picture. If you are like me, and don't process auditory input quickly, you may seem disconnected. There were times early in my marriage when my wife would ask me, "What did I just say?" On a good day I could make up some odd story and make her laugh. On other days, she would stop talking to me. I suspect she thought something like this: "Why should I talk to you when you don't care enough to listen?"

You can sharpen your listening skills by being intentional and active in the communication process. If you want to get the essence of what your partner is trying to convey to you:

- Square up.

- Make eye contact.

- Show body language that conveys that you are listening.

- Be patient.

- Don't interrupt.

- Listen with the intention to understand.

- Ask questions for more complete understanding.

- Reflect back in your own words what you are hearing.

- Acknowledge when you understand.

- Acknowledge when you *don't* understand.

- Ask your partner to explain what you don't understand.

- Return your attention when it drifts and admit when you missed something.

- Listen to your partner instead of your own thoughts.

As you continue to listen, observe the picture that is starting to form. If you think in pictures like I do, you must be patient and allow the picture to unfold. Let your partner help. The picture will unfold, and your partner will appreciate your attentiveness and effort. *"Tell me more"* conveys that you want to understand your mate's experience.

As pieces of the puzzle begin to form a picture that you can see, your partner will know when you're getting it. Through the listening connection, she will feel valued. Otherwise, when your attention drifts, she feels devalued. The same rules apply to our children. The next time your child tells you that you don't understand, believe it, and then listen actively. You will *have* influence when you *allow* influence.

Listening is a reciprocal gift.

Your family and your partner deserve to be heard, as they should be if you want to partner with them. Make this your golden rule: *Listen to others as you would have them listen to you.* When you listen deeply to others, you discover the treasures inside of them. You find the gold when you look for it.

Studs Terkel knew how to dig for gold. An oral historian, he interviewed people from all walks of life. Before reading his work, I didn't anticipate that interviews with ordinary people would be especially interesting. But he never interviewed an ordinary person. I don't believe he thought of anyone as ordinary. He looked for gold in everyone and found it. People talked to him because he was a respectful listener. Respectful listening benefits both, the speaker and the listener. It is a reciprocal gift.

A routine of daily meditation practice can enhance your ability to listen deeply and be aware of your own distracting thoughts as they arise. It can help you learn to return your attention more quickly from distractions to the words of the speaker. Just as you can condition your body through exercise, you can train your brain through a dedicated practice of meditation. See chapter ten for resources on getting started with guided meditation exercises.

Mindful Speaking

The flip side of attentive listening is mindful speaking. Like mindful listening, it requires awareness of the other person. To speak mindfully is to be thoughtful of how others hear you. You may blurt things out and hurt someone's feelings before you know it. You might bring up topics that others consider private or inappropriate to the situation. My wife tells me there are certain topics that should not be brought up at the dinner table. She no longer has to use words to shush me. She has a certain look that says, "Keep a lid on it!"

To speak mindfully, you should consider first that there is a listener. Your listener is not just an audience for your performance, but someone who would like to participate in the conversation. If you go on for long without allowing the other person to speak, they will not want to spend much time with you. They may be entertained for a while, but eventually they will feel disregarded, perhaps even disrespected. They will be worn out. When you get lost in your thoughts while speaking, and venture down many loosely-related trails, you are losing awareness of the listener. When you lose awareness, you fail to read cues that the listener is getting bored, trying to speak, or trying to get away.

To the mindless speaker, the listener's responses may feel like interruptions. The speaker's difficulty shifting attention from his thoughts to the listener's responses creates inequality in the exchange. The speaker can appear not to care that the listener has something to say, although the inattention is a symptom and not a measure of the speaker's regard. Nonetheless, the listener feels disregarded. If the listener is your relationship partner, you are likely to hear something like this: "You don't care about me!" Innocently, you wonder where that notion came from. You may wish to be understood and forgiven for your inattention, but even though the slight is unintentional, it still hurts your partner and the relationship.

Before expecting forgiveness, you need to understand your ADHD and its effects. Difficulty shifting between selective attention (required in organizing your thoughts) and open awareness (necessary for awareness of others), is typical for adults with ADHD. Put simply, you are at risk for being too focused on what you are saying and not notice if you are connecting with the listener. You may be excluding the listener and making that person feel unimportant. You might have lost friends that way. The sad part is this: You might not have a clue as to what happened.

Have a point; it makes it so much more interesting to the listener!

In the 1980s movie, *Planes, Trains, and Automobiles*, John Candy's character is a mindless chatterbox whose job is selling shower curtain rings. He has little to say of interest to his accidental traveling companion, played by Steve Martin. The viewer has little sympathy for John Candy's character until Steve Martin gets fed up and loses his composure: "Didn't you even notice on the plane when you started talking, eventually I started reading the vomit bag? Didn't that give you some kind of clue? Like, 'Hey, maybe this guy's not enjoying it?'" He ends his tirade with a suggestion: "And by the way, when you're telling these little stories, here's a good idea: Have a point! It makes it so much more interesting to the listener!"

You might begin with a point in mind, and then take so long to get to it that you forget your destination along the way, like a bridge to nowhere. I knew someone who had a remarkable ability to retrieve her main point by going into reverse, linking the most recent thought to the one before it, and then the one before that, step by step, until she arrived at where she started. Then she would say, "Oh yes, now I know what I was talking about." She was phenomenal. Most of us haven't mastered that. And even if you could do what she did, you might still be losing the listener while detouring down the trails.

You can learn to convey your thoughts efficiently, but it won't be easy for you, at least initially. You cannot learn efficient speech by thinking more about your thoughts while you are speaking. That is part of the problem. Trying to be concise and on point can be challenging and exhausting for you because of your difficulty organizing your thoughts. Every thought seems important, and so you probably say far more than necessary.

A meditation practice can help you, but you can't meditate in the middle of a conversation. Mental conditioning is like physical training that you do routinely. You wouldn't stop in the middle of a tennis match to practice a different form for your backhand. You do that in a designated time for practice. Likewise, the practice of learning mindful speaking involves a routine of awareness training. Awareness is simple—simply noticing without any judgment of what you are noticing. Thinking is complex—evaluating everything, anticipating the listener's response, thinking about your thoughts, judging the listener, judging yourself. Did you ever consider that your own brain can be your biggest source of distraction?

When you speak mindlessly, you might say whatever comes into your mind. When you do that, your thoughts will be loosely connected, and you may drift away from the topic at hand. If you try to stay on topic by *thinking* about how you are talking while you are talking, you may lose the thread altogether. How often have you asked your listener, "Now what was I talking about?" By practicing mindfulness routinely, and exercising simple awareness of the listener and awareness of the self, you can learn to convey your thoughts more clearly and with fewer words. The practice requires disciplined effort. A meditation teacher, or a mindfulness-based cognitive therapist, can help you practice observing your external and internal worlds without judgment, without becoming attached in thought to what you are observing. *Just noticing* is a skill that you can cultivate.

You may not believe that you dominate conversations, that you give more detail than necessary, or that you disregard cues from the listener who is getting bored or trying to talk. Maybe you don't think you do those things, but it won't hurt you to be open to the possibility as you observe yourself. Seek feedback from your spouse, or a close friend who will be honest with you. Dominating conversations disconnects you from the listener, and it is disrespectful. In a respectful exchange, the speaker is never more important than the listener.

While working on this chapter, a phone call interrupted my writing. I was glad to hear from my brother, who was traveling. He had something important he wanted to share, and I had some interesting things I wanted to tell him. The connection from his mobile phone was tenuous. I don't know how long I kept talking after we lost the connection, but I noticed eventually and called him back. It has happened before. We joke that I don't need a listener to keep talking. He can tolerate my excessive chatter on those occasions, as he doesn't have to hear me when we become disconnected! When I have finally stopped talking, and I hear dead air on the phone, I'm reminded that I have this problem.

Van Gogh painted *Wheatfield with Crows* with a limited number of bold strokes.

Are you sometimes vague and choppy in your speech patterns? Midway through a sentence, do you get ahead of yourself and skip forward to the next thought before completing your first sentence? Is trying to follow you like playing a scrambled word game where the listener has to construct a coherent picture from incomplete sentences? If the listener has to work so hard, he might begin to avoid conversations with you. Another problem you may have is giving every little detail that comes to mind when telling a story. When you speak mindlessly, you don't pick up on cues that the listener is getting restless, wishing to participate in the conversation or wanting to get away from you. Consider this:

- Slow down the pace of speaking so you don't get ahead of yourself and lose the listener.

- Be aware that not every thought has to be spoken in order to convey a picture.

- Remember that Van Gogh painted *Wheatfield with Crows* with a limited number of bold strokes, but you still get the picture. Get it?

Harsh Speech

Are you moody? Co-existing conditions are the rule and not the exception for adults with ADHD. Problems with emotion regulation are common to adults with ADHD and will be discussed in more detail in Chapter Nine. Your moodiness could be a function of the ADHD or a co-existing depression. The combination of "unintentional narcissism" and a mood disorder can contribute to intense and harsh speech. You might see your moodiness if only you were not in it, just as you could see a body of water if only your head were not submerged in it.

When you are in an irritable state, you are seeing *through the lens* of your mood, but you don't necessarily see the *mood*. Your brain directs your attention to the annoying person or a frustrating situation, instead of your irritable mood. Your brain is telling you that you will feel better when that person stops annoying you, or when that situation changes for the better. But once you have trained your brain to observe your emotional state (the lens itself) and drop the judgment (of the person or situation), your reasoning mind will not be so easily hijacked by your emotionally reactive mind. You will not be bothering yourself so much about what other people may be doing, or about situations that you can't control, like bad drivers on the freeway! Leave those bad drivers alone! Drop the judgment! Who are you to say there shouldn't be any bad drivers on the road? How much has your angry reaction contributed to changing that reality?

Momentary shifts in your emotional state are normal. Letting go of judgment includes not judging your brain's normal functions. If you can just notice your brain's sudden arousal, and then take a breath and let go of your story line (e.g., *There shouldn't be any bad drivers on the road!*), your brain will calm down in seconds rather than minutes, like a wave that rises and subsides.

You might not perceive your emotional state with objectivity until you are out of that state. If your vision has been corrected, you probably didn't know how poor your vision was before the correction. You might not know how inattentive you have been until you have taken ADHD medication. Depressed individuals usually don't know how depressed they have been until they are no longer depressed, as when their antidepressant medication kicks in. A loving partner or friend may be willing to share their observations about your emotional state, or the state of your attentiveness. Listen non-defensively, and thank the observer for her feedback. Willingness to listen—with respectful consideration of what you hear—can help you. If you can listen mindfully and accept feedback without defensiveness or self-loathing, your willingness will enhance the quality of your life.

KEY POINTS TO PONDER:

- You can appear selfish when lost in your limited sphere of awareness. Whatever your intentions, you are responsible for how your behavior affects others.

- Defensiveness is one way of trying not to have uncomfortable feelings.

- Listen to others as you would have them listen to you.

- If you go on for long without allowing others to speak, they will not want to spend much time with you.

- To live responsibly with ADHD is to work at developing new habits to compete with the old ones.

QUESTIONS FOR REFLECTION:

- What does it mean to look for gold when listening to someone?

- What harm does defensiveness do? How can you prevent being defensive?

- What is the relevance of Van Gogh's Wheatfield with Crows to speaking concisely?

Chapter Four

Bonds and Binds: ADHD in Relationships

I had never seen Eleanor so calm as the last time she and Paul came to my office. Paul is an athletic-looking man with a thick crop of brown and gray hair, Eleanor a petite woman with white hair and blue eyes. These two bright, independent seniors have separate hobbies and interests, but they share an active social life with close friends. Paul insists that exercise is his best medication for ADHD. He continues to work full time and enjoys playing clarinet in a community jazz orchestra. Eleanor, a retired counselor and educator, volunteers with her church and teaches high school classes to prisoners. Both give away much of their time in service to others. In the past, she had complained often that they coped with Paul's ADHD by leading mostly separate lives.

But on this day Eleanor walked into my office with a half smile. I had not seen this face before. Paul was relaxed and less defensive than normal. They were tired from having just returned from a trip to see their grandchildren. Eleanor's usual criticism of Paul's inattentiveness was noticeably absent. She had already stopped bugging him about medicine and agreed that nothing he had tried seemed to make much difference.

With her eyes closed, and with no hint of resentment in her voice, Eleanor said, "I guess I just have to accept that some of these things are never going to change. I have to change my expectations." She was ready to relieve herself of the suffering she had experienced from years of desperately holding on to an unrealized, and perhaps unrealistic, vision. This was not the first time she expressed the unlikelihood of changes she desired, but the first time I heard her convey it with acceptance—directly to Paul—instead of resentment.

In the previous meeting, Paul had expressed himself more assertively than before. With resolve, instead of his usual resignation, he had told her that she seldom acknowledged his efforts in response to her complaints. He was facing her, speaking directly to her rather than to me. His assertiveness was a big step forward for him, as his pattern had been to retreat into silence.

He disliked conflict. Eleanor had cried as she listened. It was the first time I had seen her cry. With no harshness in her voice, she told Paul that she thought she had been acknowledging his efforts. Paul calmly and confidently shared his different observation. Without either retreating or fighting, he explained that her criticisms far outnumbered her acknowledgements. She was making more withdrawals than deposits in their emotional bank account, so to speak.

By allowing her husband's influence, Eleanor was not giving up power. She was too bright and resourceful to be dependent or submissive. Instead, she was giving more power to the relationship, as was Paul. He was stepping up, and she was stepping back. Each partner was finding personal power and "partnership competence" in a new way. They began to speak about activities that they enjoy together. In the past, they had more often spoken about their separate interests, as if they were symbols of hopelessness and resignation. On this occasion they talked about Paul's eventual retirement and how they had recently begun to discard possessions that they preferred not to carry into their next home. They were planning a move to Virginia. "We want to retire near the grandchildren," Eleanor said. She was envisioning their future together.

In this chapter we will explore:

- how **ADHD** affects your primary relationship

- how you and your partner can respect its presence in the relationship

- how the partnership can prevent problems that **ADHD** can create

The ADHD brain is exceptional—roughly 5 percent of all adult brains. We think we should be no different from the other 95 percent, and yet we are. Consequently, we enter relationships with unrealistic expectations. Without fully understanding and embracing differences from our non-ADHD peers, we fail to access the power of acceptance and positive regard. Both partners are affected.

If an attention disorder is in the marriage, it will have an impact.

Is the following story familiar to you? When you found the love of your life, you fell deeply in love—as much with your own excitement as with your new mate. Your partner felt special to be the object of your hyper-focused attention. But when novelty and urgency receded, the intensity of your passion faded. You began to show less interest, and you were oblivious to your partner's loss of your attention. When she expressed hurt and disappointment, you felt criticized and diminished. Rather than attend to her, you defended yourself and then retreated. Thus, a pattern of criticism and defensiveness was born. Blame began to chip away at the foundation. Traditional country music made millions on the theme of lost passion. Conway Twitty had a hit in the 1970s with L. E. White's song, "After the Fire Is Gone": "There's nothing cold as ashes after the fire is gone."

However your relationship began, ADHD will remain a player. If an attention disorder is in the marriage, it will have an impact. But unlike other disabilities, ADHD is not all that visible. You can see evidence of physical disabilities. When my wife needs to remove the lid from a jar, she hands it to me. I can see clearly how her wrists, weakened by rheumatoid arthritis, are affected by her disability. I remove the lid and hand the jar back to her with little thought. The exchange has become automatic. My cognitive disability is less visible, but the same partnering attitude helps us prevent the ADHD from creating avoidable problems. When we need to file a receipt, I hand the receipt to her before I have a chance to misplace it, and she files it. My difficulty keeping track of items and maintaining order could be misperceived as not being concerned about our finances, when in fact I care enough not to risk losing receipts! I would never tell her that she doesn't mind interrupting me when she hands me a jar to open, and she never tells me that I don't care about our finances. Neither is true.

The vast majority of ADHD couples enter their relationship clueless about the ADHD and its effects, and so the reasons for their dysfunctional interactions remain a mystery. Incorrect interpretations lead to hurt feelings and contentious communication. The ADHD partner's inconsistent attention and poor working memory are perceived as lack of caring.

If I don't allow enough time to get ready for an event that is important to my wife, I can seem unconcerned about her need to be prompt, especially if I get sidetracked onto something that is important only to me. My attention can get so stuck that I appear selfish. When she takes care of herself around my ADHD, she gently reminds me that I need to start getting ready. I thank her. She knows that I don't consider reminders to be nagging or parenting me. I have encouraged her to protect herself from being inconvenienced by my ADHD. I consider her prompts to be acts of generosity. They help both of us, and we prefer partnering to blaming. To be competent relationship partners, it is necessary for both individuals to respect the presence of ADHD in the marriage. My wife once expressed sympathy for how her rheumatoid arthritis affects me. But I'm the lucky one; I don't have to carry the pain and unpredictable flair-ups in my body. Like my ADHD, her RA is a reality in our marriage. I know she feels the same because she made that comparison once in a presentation at my ADHD couples workshop.

Adults with ADHD are often accused of not caring, and yet I have met mostly sensitive and loving people in my support group. They are spirited, creative individuals who are willing to take risks, and those qualities are part of what attracted their partners. They are also distractible and forgetful, and they interrupt others, arrive late for events, misplace things, drive too fast, lose track in conversations, and make mindless mistakes from their inattention. Most of them are both adorable and frustrating to their partners. When the inattention dominates a relationship, the non-ADHD partner forgets the positive qualities.

Too much demolition makes rebuilding difficult.

Here is what ADHD couples look like when the effects of ADHD in the marriage are present and not understood, especially when the dynamics have been years in the making:

"You act like a child. We have two children already, and I don't need a third."

"Then stop talking to me as if I *am* a child."

"If I didn't stay on you, nothing would change and nothing would get done."

"If you would stop nagging, we could be happy. You need to lighten up."

"I'm not going to let you off the hook. ADHD is no excuse for your irresponsibility."

"You act like my mother and then expect me to be intimate with you."

"I give up!" (...*until the next offense.*)

"I will no longer fight with you!" (...*until you flush me out of my cave again.*)

If understanding and acceptance are cornerstones of a healthy relationship, then ignorance and blame are tremors that crack the foundation. Persistent fighting and retreating are destructive. Too much demolition makes rebuilding difficult. Prevention—not punishment—is the key. Prevention of problems that ADHD can cause means using strategies and developing new habits to compete with old patterns. It requires effort by *both* partners.

I have helped couples with undiagnosed ADHD discover, and understand, the card that has been missing from the deck. The work can be difficult with couples who have spent years practicing criticism and defensiveness. For a relationship to succeed with ADHD, both partners must take a leap of faith and jump together. Criticizing, blaming, berating, being defensive, retreating, and resigning can only poison a relationship.

But stopping the bleeding is not enough. You have reason to aim higher than just good enough. Good enough is not enough! Who wants to live with their heads barely above water? Bufflehead ducks spend hours diving under water and floating on the surface, but they can also fly!

For several years I have led workshops for couples dealing with ADHD. I have learned much from participants, especially in an inner-outer circle exercise. In that one-hour exercise, spouses of ADHD partners sit in a circle, facing one another and discussing what it is like to be in a partnership with someone who has ADHD. The ADHD partners are behind them in an outer circle, listening to this discussion. Those in the outer circle are not allowed to speak. After twenty minutes, the circles switch. The ADHD partners become the discussants in the inner circle, and the non-ADHD partners become the observers. The ADHD partners discuss how they experience their relationships. After each group has had its turn, the entire group discusses what they learned. Often, participants say they never realized there were other couples like them, and they didn't fully understand their partner's experiences until they heard the stories of couples with similar challenges. It is a new beginning. Those who had been in couple therapy before, but without understanding the effects of ADHD in the partnership, leave with a clearer vision of what can be. No longer the "experts" on their partner's motives, they can re-invest in their relationship with a beginner's mind where they are open to learning more from each other.

The workshop groups are usually diverse. There are couples where both partners have attention disorders. There are same-sex couples and couples of mixed ethnicity. And there are couples with different cultural heritages. The diversity enriches our discussions. We are all different in some important ways, and we are all the same. Mutual respect empowers our partnerships.

Melissa Orlov, author of *The ADHD Effect on Marriage*, challenges both partners. She understands that there are more possibilities when both partners take responsibility for changing their own behavior patterns and then work together as partners to change the partnership. Orlov is the non-ADHD partner in her marriage. What I found most valuable in Orlov's book is her description of a pattern in ADHD couples that may be universal:

Symptom ➤ response ➤ response (to the response)[8]

I can best illustrate this dynamic with a personal example, from long before my wife and I learned effective ways to partner with my ADHD. She called me at work one evening and asked when I would be coming home. She was not satisfied with my answer. I expected to work late, which was not unusual. "Kevin and Susan are here and we are waiting on you to begin dinner," she said. "Oh!" I replied, genuinely surprised. "You didn't tell me they were coming" (which was unlikely, considering they were driving six hours from St. Louis to Nashville). "I've been telling you all week," she said, annoyed. "No you didn't," I responded defensively. "That is something I know I would have remembered."

My wife was slow to recover from her frustration with me that evening, even though I rushed home. She wasn't saying much to me. I began to feel angry at her for being angry at me. After all, I was innocent...so I thought. I had begun feeling sorry for myself, the poor victim of his wife's anger. The truth is, she deserved understanding and acceptance for the effect of *my* problem— my unreliable memory. Instead, I was thinking, "I'm not such a bad person. My unintended offense did not warrant an angry response." I may as well have said, "You should always overlook my forgetfulness, no matter how it affects you and our guests." Really?

Now, here are the facts:

I forgot (symptom) ➤ She was rightfully angry (response) ➤ I became angry that she was angry (response to the response).

Framing this as a pattern is helpful. It feels less personal when the pattern is understood to be common to ADHD couples. If I had dropped my defensiveness and listened to the injured party, my wife would have recovered more quickly from her rightful anger. And if I had apologized immediately and demonstrated understanding, she still would have been frustrated, but she would have felt understood and her recovery would have been easy and quick. Frustrated and understood is better than frustrated and disregarded.

> To learn about Melissa Orlov's *ADHD Effect Couple's Seminar,* an 8-week course you can attend in the comfort of your home by phone, go to www.adhdmarriage.com.

To acknowledge is to demonstrate respect, which is essential to relationship competence. Admitting responsibility can feel like admitting incompetence, but it is a noble and generous act. There is no reason for shame in having a memory problem. You are more likely to learn from your experiences when you acknowledge truth and demonstrate compassion—for your partner and yourself. Accepting a complaint is taking a strong position, and is far more productive than either defensiveness or self-loathing. Self-loathing is pointless and destructive. Being human, you have not gone beyond the capacity to make mistakes and cause pain, just as you have not gone beyond the capacity to grow old and die.

John Gottman's research on healthy and unhealthy relationships highlights four particular problems that are most destructive of marriages: criticism, contempt, stonewalling (shutting down), and defensiveness. Other marriage experts cite contempt as the most harmful of the four. Contempt refers less to intention than effect. You might not intend to roll your eyes, exhale loudly, or look dumbfounded, but doing so has a big effect. A contemptuous posture conveys to your partner that he or she is inferior, stupid, or unlovable. Whether you express contempt verbally or nonverbally, you may as well be saying, "You are too stupid to comprehend." Contempt is hurtful and does nothing but harm the relationship. It arouses strong emotion in your partner. And when a brain is flooded with emotion, it is temporarily incapable of reasoning.

If you are so angry that you wish your partner to feel it, you are likely to flood her brain with strong emotion. She will be angry at you in return. Good luck partnering under those conditions! Two emotionally reactive brains can do a lot of harm to a partnership. The emotionally flooded brain has to recover before the reasoning brain can come back online and resume the work of partnering. A more useful direction is to help your partner feel safe and respected. If you are the target of your partner's contempt, tell her that you don't think she would intentionally try to hurt you, and ask her to express what she needs to tell you in some other way.

Here are some tips for making an ADHD partnership work:

For the ADHD partner –

1. Get professional help for living well with ADHD.

2. Learn and practice the skill of mindful listening.

3. Square up and allow your partner's influence.

4. Join a support group to learn and share successful strategies.

5. Learn how not to react defensively.

6. Remember why you chose your partner.

7. Tell your partner what you like about her.

8. Stop nagging your mate about nagging. Be grateful for helpful prompts.

9. Commit to learning how to partner effectively around the ADHD in your marriage.

For the non-ADHD partner –

1. Learn all you can about your partner's ADHD and brain differences.

2. Don't be the expert on your partner's motives.

3. Replace harsh criticisms with requests.

4. Express appreciation for your partner's positive qualities.

5. Learn how to lighten up. Pressure makes ADHD symptoms worse.

6. Encourage your ADHD partner to get help; don't try to be your mate's therapist.

7. Expect your partner to be responsible despite the ADHD. If one strategy doesn't work, suggest trying another way rather than trying harder.

8. Don't act superior, as if your partner is broken and you are whole.

9. Commit to learning how to partner effectively around the ADHD in your marriage.

KEY POINTS TO PONDER:

- Without fully embracing differences from our non-ADHD peers, we fail to access the power of acceptance and positive regard. Both partners are affected.

- However your relationship began, ADHD will remain a player.

- To be competent relationship partners, both individuals must respect the presence of ADHD in the marriage.

- Too much demolition makes rebuilding difficult. Prevention means developing new habits to compete with old patterns, which requires mercy and commitment to change.

- Admitting responsibility can feel like admitting incompetence, but it is a noble and generous act. It demonstrates respect, an essential ingredient in a competent partnership.

QUESTIONS FOR REFLECTION:

- When your partner expresses hurt or disappointment, do you feel empathy, or do you feel criticized and diminished? Do you move toward your partner or away? Do you allow influence or defend and retreat?

- Why are adults with ADHD often accused by their partners of not caring?

- What is the inner-outer circle exercise in the ADHD couples workshop? Can you think of two reasons that relationship partners might listen better in the exercise than at home?

- Can you think of a personal example that illustrates Melissa Orlov's description of the symptom → response → response dynamic?

Chapter Five

Unplugging

Imagine that you have two appliances, a radio and a reading light, plugged into a two-receptacle outlet behind your bedside table. You want to charge your phone while you read in bed. You need the light for reading, but you don't need the radio, and so you unplug the radio to free up an outlet for the phone. Attention management is like this. You often have to unplug your hyperfocused attention from one activity in order to plug it into another. The compromised attention manager in your ADHD brain resists unplugging. That resistance is why you feel annoyed when your spouse tells you to stop reading your email and get dressed so you can leave the house on time for an outing. Before you can get dressed, you have to stop reading your email. When your attention is locked into a focused state, it wants to stay there. Opening up your awareness is necessary for shifting to another activity, just like unplugging your radio allows you to plug in your phone.

You can get so absorbed in an activity that you become oblivious to everything and everyone else. Just ask your spouse or an honest friend if that is true. The difficulty you have with unplugging interferes with the broader awareness of time and competing priorities. Before getting dressed, you believed that you had plenty of time. Checking your email messages would take "no time at all," and so you replied to two of them, which took ten minutes. Then, after you shifted back from selective attention to open awareness and looked at the clock, you wondered where the time went. The time didn't go anywhere! Your open awareness went somewhere! Your attention was plugged into a low-priority activity.

This chapter is about awareness of awareness. If you turn the lights up on how your ADHD affects you, you can stop stumbling around in the dark. You can practice unplugging from activities, thoughts, and destructive habits that waste your time.

In this chapter I will address how to unplug your ADHD brain from:

- habitual mindlessness
- hyperfocus

- thoughts

- time-wasters

- destructive indulgence

- excuses

Unplugging from Habitual Mindlessness

Let's say you are a songwriter, and you have an idea for a song. You want to get into the flow of it while you have the idea in mind. If you don't write it now, you might forget the idea. So, you begin writing. You try not to edit as you write your first draft in order to get into "the zone" and remain there. The zone feels good. Nothing else exists in the world right now except those words on the page and the melody coming from your piano. You complete the lyric and start recording the melody on your digital recorder before you forget what's in your head. There is nothing in the world but your song in this moment. You brain is locked in, and awareness of any other obligation is suspended.

As if jolted by thunder out of a deep sleep, something triggers a memory: you were going to make a deposit at the bank and pay bills before starting to write. You hadn't glanced at the clock even once and you failed to make the deposit before the bank closed. You had begun the day with plenty of time to do everything you needed to do, and so you felt no need to prioritize and schedule your tasks. You entered "the zone" and left the world. When your open awareness returned, the bank was closed and your wife was angry at you for being so irresponsible...again!

Does this story illustrate a deficit of attention, an excess of attention, or an attention-management problem? Preparing a deposit and paying bills would have required you to activate your selective attention. But shifting into focus on one task required pulling back from focusing on another. Attention management was the real problem.

Awareness of competing priorities happens when your awareness is open rather than focused. This creates a paradox for attention management: you may not be aware of how focused you are when focused. You must wake up first to direct your attention. Just as an alarm clock is a tool that shifts your state of unconsciousness to conscious, you can use tools—like reminders on your smart phone—to gently open your awareness.

You can learn, through practice, how to hold your attention in place and how to open your awareness. A *focused* type of meditation—as in focusing on the breath or a mantra—can enhance your ability to activate and sustain your selective attention, whereas an *open awareness* type of meditation—as in observing sounds or rising thoughts—can help you develop the skill of observing and redirecting your attention. Being stuck in a focused state is an understated form of mindlessness. A common misperception about ADHD is that it is nothing more than an inability to focus. You were told in school to be attentive to the task at hand, to be focused. But you also needed to be aware of others, mindful of purpose, conscious of priorities, and open to creative ideas.

After a day of seeing psychotherapy clients, if I plunge into writing notes immediately, I will work in circles. I may write one note, return one call, write a referral letter, begin to log procedure codes and payments, and then return to writing notes. I will waste time in a disorderly transition from one activity to the next. I call it spinning. When I take a few minutes to be silent first, I can proceed more efficiently. My brain's attention manager is better prepared, when I relax into a more open state, to notice when I am about to start spinning. I can then redirect my attention to the priority at hand.

Awareness of the *inclination* to spin is, in effect, awareness of your state of awareness. Mindfulness training can improve that kind of open awareness.

You don't have to become a meditating monk to be better at unplugging. This morning I got up at sunrise to walk the trails at

Radnor Lake, a wonderful refuge just four miles from my house. Despite how close it is, I sometimes forget the park is there. I try to go without a purpose, other than to be mindfully present and alert to my surroundings. Sometimes I take my camera, which helps me remain attentive to the beauty all around me, rather than to what is spinning in my mind.

There were times in the past when I would go to the lake to get away from something stressful. I would walk with mindless speed, as if running from something. I was trying to extinguish the dark and difficult parts of life that were filling up my small mind so I could have some open space and light in it. But trying to rid myself of negative thoughts and difficulties, and then failing to do so, only generated *more* negative thoughts.

Life can be dark and difficult. I'm sorry, but life is just like that sometimes. Trying to make it some other way is impossible and will get you stuck in your small mind, focusing on nothing else but what you wish not to be experiencing. Expanding your awareness is a better way to have more light. This simple truth can be liberating: *Life is much bigger than your negative thoughts, and always has been.* Beauty surrounds you, but you have to open your eyes—your awareness—to see it.

You may not be in a work environment that allows opportunities to take a walk or a brief meditation break while on the clock. But a daily mindfulness routine at home, if only for ten minutes in the morning, will enhance your ability to stop, breathe, and reset your attention when you need to—at work or anywhere else, any time of day or night.

Individuals in my ADHD support group often share resourceful ways that they unplug from mindlessness. Here are a few strategies they have contributed:

- A divorced woman invites a friend over to sit on her sofa and read while she cleans her house. Having someone in the house prevents her from mindlessly spinning or becoming obsessively focused on just one task.

- A business owner uses a recurring alert on his phone, and a spiral notepad with his list of priorities for the day, and revisits his priorities at timed intervals.

- One individual stopped subscribing to the daily newspaper except for weekends.

- One man's supportive wife calls out his name when he drifts from the task at hand, and he thanks her when she does so.

- An executive uses a large mechanical one-hour timer which he simply resets repeatedly. He explains that seeing a visual representation of the passing of time helps him to stay mindful that minutes become hours. It helps him not waste time.

- A few participants have studied and practiced insight meditation as a means to observing internal and external events with less distracting mental activity and without judgment.

Unplugging from Brainlock

Lee went to therapy for a family crisis and ended up with an ADHD diagnosis. The family crisis was precipitated by his having been hyperfocused on work and hobbies throughout much of his marriage. He had become a virtual stranger to his wife and children. For better *and* for worse, he was extraordinarily successful with his businesses and fulfilled by his many hobbies. As he described it, he spent much of his time in "the rabbit hole" where he was immersed in his private world. His wife had the strength to function independently for many years and tried not to need what was missing in the marriage. When she would get angry, he would just spend more time in his cave. He learned early in life how to make money and was good at it. A competent provider, he became skilled at starting businesses and knowing when to sell them. He learned how to use information technology effectively, and he had many interesting hobbies. He worked from home, a large home that allowed ample office space (what he called his "rabbit hole").

Lee had assumed for years that being productive meant remaining in the hole until he finished what he was doing. He would often remain there well into the evening. His family would see very little of him for days at a time.

Eventually, his marriage hit a wall, and the crisis jolted him from the comfort of his hole. He would have to make radical changes or lose his family. Opening up his awareness to resume the role of husband and father would not happen overnight. It might not have happened at all if not for the independence, strength, and rightful anger of a committed partner. Strong enough to leave the marriage, she chose to stay and fight for the life she wanted with her husband. She made him listen, and he did. He promised to make radical changes, and he did. At first, she did not want to hear anything about ADHD. She was not about to allow him a forum for rationalizing his neglect. Still, she had been unaware of the role of the ADHD, like most couples before diagnosis. ADHD, in effect, had been an invisible partner in the relationship.

Their commitment to healing the relationship provided a foundation from which they would learn to be real partners. Eventually, they began to partner effectively around his ADHD. She did not become his caretaker, but learned how to take care of herself around his ADHD and redirect his attention when needed. He learned to open his eyes and see what mattered most in his life. It was right in front of him.

Lee began psychotherapy, learned about mindfulness and the ADHD brain, participated in an ADHD support group, attended an ADHD couple's workshop, and took medication that helped him manage his attention. He discovered that he could compartmentalize his work day. He began to work four hours in the morning, stop for lunch, and then work four more hours in the afternoon. He was getting his work done in less time. He took walks with his wife, sometimes in the middle of the day. Together, they created a loving relationship that was more fulfilling than what they had experienced for over twenty years. That's what they told me.

Unplugging from Thoughts

Spoken words connect us and unspoken words (thoughts) differentiate us. No one knows your unexpressed thoughts, and you don't know the unexpressed thoughts of others. Your thoughts and images can be so complex and vivid that you may sometimes mistake them for absolute truths. If you are a passenger on a plane that is lifting off the runway, and you imagine it crashing, you are likely to feel the sensation of fear. Nothing has happened in reality, but something has happened in your imagination, in your mental activity. Your brain's imagining was all that scared you. Brain activity is like that. The same regions of the brain that activate in response to an event will activate much the same in response to *images* of that event. When you imagine being provoked by someone you dislike, you will likely feel the sensation of anger.

Practicing mindfulness means learning to observe thoughts, sensations, perceptions, and feelings without judging them. It allows you to discern the difference between mental activities and actual events. You can learn to stop living anxiously in your imagination and start living your life. The alternative is to squander precious moments that you will never get back. Talk to someone who has a terminal illness, or someone who has survived a close brush with death. They will tell you that all the worrying they did was a waste of time. One way not to waste time is to live in the time that you have.

When you stop living in your head, you can square up and listen deeply to others. You can experience them more fully. They might not recognize exactly what has changed in you, but they will notice your presence. Mindful presence says to them, "You are important enough to have my undivided attention." When I am speaking to someone whose attention is drifting away, I feel abandoned in that moment. I feel disregarded and unimportant. Listening with the intention of comprehending what someone is trying to convey to you is different from listening to your thoughts about what they are saying. Anticipating, assuming, and interpreting are contrary to mindful listening. Carly Simon wrote about this in her song "Anticipation":

We can never know about the days to come

But we think about them anyway

And I wonder if I'm really with you now

Or just chasing after some finer day[9]

Unplugging from Time-wasters

You probably don't have a clue as to how much time you waste. And you probably don't realize how much you allow others to waste your time. I think most of us waste more time than we use effectively. Mindless chatter, failure to prioritize, and perpetual detours from the task at hand rob us of productivity. Jill Bolte Taylor tells us to stop saying we are wasting time because "it is a waste of time to say it."[10]

If you feel compelled to read the morning paper while drinking your coffee, you will drink coffee for forty-five minutes instead of fifteen minutes. Reading every email message consumes valuable time. Composing a perfectly written email message is a time-waster. Compulsively answering all phone calls can waste hours. Allowing someone to visit too long on the telephone is a self-inflicted time-waster. A televised football game consumes three hours. Activities on your electronic devices eat up more time than you realize when you are brainlocked in them. Your proclaimed priorities are not always your actual priorities.

Let me tell you about two individuals whose crises taught them valuable lessons about protecting their time. Derrell temporarily lost his body to paralysis, and Connie lost her brother to an unsolved homicide. Before his paralysis, Derrell too often sacrificed his time for others at the expense of his own goals. Connie had prioritized numbness over uncomfortable emotions. Both of these achievers had life experiences that woke them up. You don't have to wait for a crisis to wake up and take charge of your time and your life. But

people who have awakened that way often consider themselves
lucky, not that they had the crisis, but that they woke up.

Derrell experienced a brief part of his life with an active brain
and an inactive body that was paralyzed temporarily. He says he
now values the time that his paralysis forced on him. It allowed
him an opportunity to reflect on what was important in his life,
including life's impermanence. After he regained his mobility, he
became more assertive in prohibiting others from wasting his time.
He has no time for gossip, drama, and pointless conflicts. When
confronted with a necessary conflict, he pushes to get to the
bottom line. He invites useful criticism and directness from others,
and he expects others to respect *his* directness. If someone
misinterprets his motives, he skillfully and sensitively corrects the
misinterpretation and moves on. He is a sensitive person, but he
does not feel a disproportionate obligation to protect others from
their feelings, nor to manage what others think of him.

Connie's brother was murdered, and the killer was never
found. For years, she was obsessed with why and how this
happened. Now, she refuses to waste any more time living in her
head. She would rather live in her life. Emerging from years of
obsessing over her brother's mysterious death, and believing that
she was an expert on grieving, she shifted her focus to conscious
living and wrote a book about it.[11] She brings a playful spirit to her
relationship with a partner who is as organized as Connie is
disorganized. They have learned to partner effectively around
Connie's ADHD, and they are successful real estate brokers. Connie
is an author, blogger, podcaster, realtor, and "parent" to her aging
mother. She practices meditation routinely, and she gets things
done. Like Derrell, she has learned not to waste time worrying
about what she cannot control, including what others think of her.
She told the ADHD support group that she has adopted the
philosophy of "what you think of me is none of my business."[12]

Unplugging from Destructive Indulgence

In his early adulthood, Josh sometimes felt more focused when
using alcohol or marijuana. The experience was inconsistent,

however, and negative effects of substance abuse eventually became bigger than perceived benefits. What he initially experienced as mind-expanding became mind-numbing. The big box became a small box. In that small box he didn't need others, didn't need to get out of his head, didn't need to pay attention to his body, and was less attuned to the needs and feelings of others.

To those who insist there is no harm in using, I often ask if they are achieving their goals and if their effort is matching their aspirations. They are seldom working as hard as they think, and they are often falling short of actualizing their vision.

I asked Josh whether he thought he should live a life of sobriety if not moderation. "Yes, of course I should," he replied. He was knowledgeable about the health risks of abusing alcohol and drugs. He had been living in a fantasy world of achievement and fame, and not really working all that hard. He was experiencing competing truths: (1) He saw in himself a creative person when using drugs, and (2) because of drug use, he wasted years before his efforts began to match his aspirations. He had temporarily left the world of normal feelings, clearheaded observations, and consistent effort. Anxiety and depression had begun to derail him. Substituting mindful living for mindless indulgence got him back on track, and he began to attain some of his life goals. The happiness he attained by conscious effort trumped the temporary comforts and grandiose fantasies inspired by his alcohol and drug abuse.

Abuse of alcohol and drugs can inhibit normal brain functions that might otherwise prevent anxiety and depression. A habit of avoiding or escaping normal emotions eventually magnifies them and will obstruct you from learning to live well with them. Your emotions have a normal function. They are rooted in your biological makeup and history of experiences. And since you cannot change your history, or guarantee yourself only comfortable feelings, accepting the truth of your history and your emotional life is adaptive. Wishing not to have your history, or uncomfortable emotions, is *not* adaptive. Meditation teachers talk of "leaning into your feelings" rather than pushing back against them, as you might relax and lean into a cold wind rather than shiver. Letting go of the resistance helps you tolerate what you were resisting. Acceptance is a powerful antidote.

Willingness to feel is willingness to live.

Numbness is not a way to be safe. If you are willing to feel normal discomfort associated with living fully, then willingness is your ticket to freedom from anxiety. To be anxious about becoming anxious is to be *more* anxious, not less. Willingness to feel is willingness to live. The alternative is to avoid normal feelings for a few decades and then die so you can rest in peace. You should be less afraid of dying than *not living*. You will die only once.

As people who have embraced recovery will tell you, living one day at a time is manageable. Living one moment at a time is even *more* manageable. Addiction is a real risk for adults with ADHD. Approximately 25 percent of adults being treated for alcohol and drug abuse have ADHD.

Unplugging from Excuses

You have ADHD. So what! Deal with it! Refuse to make too much of your ADHD, and don't ever use it to rationalize underachieving. When I was a child, my mother would not tolerate my unwillingness to try something. Whenever I said, "I can't do it," she would reply, "Can't never did anything."

I tell adolescents and young adults, newly diagnosed with ADHD, never to use the disorder as an excuse for not taking responsibility for their lives. "Don't make the rest of us look bad," I insist. We have to live in the world with people—even professionals—who deny the existence of ADHD. Disregarding the evidence, they proclaim that people like us are "looking for an excuse" for irresponsibility and underachievement. I have yet to meet anyone who aspires to underachieve. It helps when others get it, but it is far more important that *you* get it. Understanding it is essential to accepting it.

Your effort must be wise effort. Telling yourself to try harder to concentrate, or to try harder to remember, is not really doing anything. Creating an ADHD-friendly environment is a more effective way to live well. Get off the sofa and put down the remote control, protect yourself from time-wasters, deal with stress skillfully, and practice unplugging from electronic devices and other mindless distractions. Wake up your brain by taking it into novel situations.

If you want to go beyond keeping your head above water and attain your life goals, you will need to be resourceful and intentional. When you are "plugged in" too much of the time, you risk being oblivious to everything outside your inner world. You will not see what you are missing, just as you don't know what your cat is doing when you are asleep. Out of sight is out of mind. On the other hand, when you open your awareness, honor your vision and your intentions, and prioritize accordingly, you will experience the joy of living well with ADHD.

KEY POINTS TO PONDER:

- The compromised attention manager in your brain resists unplugging. Opening up your awareness is necessary for shifting from one activity to another.

- "Plenty-of-time thinking" is an automatic thought that assumes you have ample time to do what you prefer to do before starting what should be your first priority.

- You can condition your brain to be better at observing your state of awareness.

- A daily routine of meditation helps you make the best of opportunities at any time to stop, breathe, and reset your attention. Like physical conditioning, brain conditioning helps you sustain your effort and also helps you unplug.

- The internal activity of your brain is not the same as external events and realities.

QUESTIONS FOR REFLECTION:

- What is an antidote for putting off studying and then cramming for an exam?

- How do you know when you are living in your mind rather than in your life?

- How do you know when you are listening deeply to someone or listening mostly to your interpretations and judgments?

- If avoiding or escaping anxious feelings immediately decreases discomfort, what is the long-term effect of avoidance? How does this relate to effects of alcohol and drug abuse?

Chapter Six

Creating

> "Imagination is more important than knowledge."
> — *Albert Einstein*

> "When I look back on all the crap I learned in high school,
> it's a wonder I can think at all."
> — *Paul Simon (from the song "Kodachrome")*

Creatively Expressing Yourself

Did you know that you may be wired for creativity? Many characteristics associated with creativity are associated with ADHD as well. One study found that college students with the ADHD diagnosis scored higher in measures of creativity than their non-ADHD peers. Another showed that adolescents with ADHD scored higher than their non-ADHD peers in measures of divergent thinking[14]. That means they were better at finding creative solutions to problems.

Chances are, you tend to think flexibly and expansively, generating ideas and creative solutions, unlike convergent thinkers who narrow options to find the correct answer. The strength in divergent thinking, found in creative people, may be related to the lack of inhibition in the ADHD population. In other words, finding creative solutions and generating ideas with spontaneity is not for the inhibited!

If you've ever attended a party for someone resigning from your workplace, you know what a delightful experience it usually is for the person leaving. Everyone has nice things to say to their outgoing colleague. When I was leaving a job in Los Angeles, one of my professional peers said this about me:

"There were times when you didn't seem to be with us during our discussions, but when you spoke up, you often synthesized all that we had been talking about and moved us forward." What I thought was ordinary might not have been. I was aware only that I was bored with too much talking, yet stimulated by the big picture.

I could have slept through one member's philosophical digressions, but would become alert when another colleague said something pertinent to the task at hand. I had less information to remember than those who were more attentive to everything they were hearing. I was not especially interested in details. Separate pieces of the puzzle were far less interesting to me than the picture that my restless mind was forming.

How would you know you're not creative?

I've heard a lot of adults with ADHD say that they are not creative. If you grew up often hearing that you are off task, that daydreaming is bad, that doodling is not allowed, that you are using the wrong color, that you should sit still and be quiet, that you should try to be like everyone else, that you cannot draw outside the lines, that clowning will be punished, that studying Latin will be good for you—then how would you know you're not creative? And like anyone, creative individuals must learn how to express their creativity, no matter what form it takes. Writers have to learn the craft of writing, musicians have to learn to read music and play their instruments, potters have to learn how to work with clay, and painters have to learn how to use their tools.

One of my ADHD support group members likes to draw, and he is very talented. Friends tell him he could make money with this talent. He tells them that if he thought about drawing for money, he would stop enjoying it. He likes the process of creating. There is no outcome to which he aspires that can get in his way of experiencing joy in creating. This may be the reason we often like the first album of our favorite performing artist. First songs are written more freely, and by writers who are unconcerned about realistic goals. They are experiencing the joy of creating something from the heart.

I was lucky to have a mother who always encouraged me. I was unlucky that she made me believe I could do *anything*. I knew nothing about sustaining effort. I started far more projects and activities than I completed. And now I know that individuals with ADHD have problems sustaining effort and completing one task before starting the next. Thomas Edison started many experiments and inventions at once. He didn't always complete one before going on to the next, but his creativity and productivity were extraordinary. I'm told that in one year he obtained more than fifty new patents, which means he averaged nearly one per week.

I never thought I was creative until well into adulthood. I lacked patience. I had limited capacity for sustaining effort and no understanding of why I was different from my peers. They seemed to be creative with little effort. At age twenty-eight I moved from Nashville to Los Angeles. I became lonely and depressed after several months, living alone there. I tried to find some kind of class that would put me in contact with other people. I needed friends. I went to the first class of Beginner's Bridge one night at a community center, one block from my apartment in Santa Monica. Everyone there knew how to play already! I dropped out immediately. Beach volleyball classes were available only during weekdays, when I was at work. Writing classes at UCLA Extension were taught mostly during the day. But I found a song lyric writing class there that met weekly on Tuesday evenings for ten weeks. I signed up.

The teacher, Buddy Kaye, was a white-haired man whose songwriting successes were mostly in the 1940s and early 1950s. His peers were some of the greatest songwriters who ever lived. Frank Sinatra recorded one of his biggest hit songs. Buddy was brutal. He told us the first night that we would bring a complete original lyric each week and read it in front of the class. That first night he instructed us on how to write a good title. We would learn to write lyrics from a "hook" that was represented in the title. He directed us to write three titles that night in the classroom, and he would pick the best of the three. Our first assignment would be to write a lyric from the selected title. After all the other students read their titles out loud, and the teacher chose the best of the three, I raised my hand to tell him he had overlooked me.

"Oh, alright," he grumbled, and waved his hand dismissively in my direction. "Read yours." He didn't look at me while I was reading them. I was proud of my titles and happy to read them aloud.

"I don't like any of them," he said. "Just use the last one." He quickly moved on to talk about our first assignment. I would have to write a lyric from a title that he didn't like. I was not surprised when he didn't like the lyric that I brought to the next class. I was certain he didn't like me for some reason, but I continued attending. By the third class, I was still intimidated by him, but encouraged that I could write an entire lyric, while the majority of students were writing no more than a few lines. It helped me to observe that all of us, except maybe one student, were equally displeasing him.

I was afraid that I would not find any good ideas for class number three. Nothing worth writing was coming from my anxious brain or my cluttered apartment. I wasn't going to find my lyric there. So I drove to Ole Mahoney's Irish Whip on Main Street in Santa Monica one evening, in search of a story that I could embellish into a song lyric. I would treat myself to live music and beer. Hot Licks and Finger Tips were playing Western swing. The bar separated the music area from the back where patrons played pool and foosball. Two women playing foosball suckered me, and one other innocent man, into playing a game with them. We gladly accepted and got whipped in every game.

Two lyrics came from embellishing that evening. I wrote a third before the week was up, because I was afraid of my teacher. I took two complete lyrics to the next class, and Mr. Intimidating let me read both. I was surprised by applause from my classmates when I finished reading them. They were not marketable songs, understand, and my peers were not publishers, but my teacher softened a bit toward me after that response from the class. The best outcome of that class was gaining a friend for life, the one student who never seemed to displease the teacher. Mike Himelstein was the success story in our class. He would go on to write hit songs and tunes for television and movies.

At the end of our ten-week course, the teacher asked four of us to remain after class. He thought we had potential for success and said we should continue meeting as a small group to critique each other's work. We continued to enjoy writing and learning for several months. I have no regrets for never having written a hit song, or earning no income from songwriting. I had one song performed one night in a club in Nashville, thanks to my brother who knew the singer! Still, creating songs was always gratifying.

After I moved back from Los Angeles to Nashville, my teacher would travel to Music City on occasion to work with some local songwriters. Sometimes he would take me to dinner or to a recording session. After Jim Chappell and I landed a contract with a major publisher for a song we co-wrote (no one ever recorded it), Buddy wrote a letter of encouragement to us. Jim would later become a successful composer and performer of piano melodies, and I have a nice letter in my files.

April 7, 1980

Dear Terry and Jim:

Was really pleased to read your collaborated letter, being sort of the Godfather to the two of you. It will even please me more when you get your first recording, which might even be this year.

But you know these things take a long time, and I know you're both mature enough not to grow impatient. Every song, every meeting, every day is a learning experience.

A couple of the Nashville songs I wrote are being

recorded. It really seems to be taking forever, and the records are not by so-called big names. That'll be the hard way. But it's a case of out of sight, out of mind. I believe I have the right songs, but do I have the runners?

At any rate, do stay in touch. I will try to be in Nashville before the year is up.

Best of luck. I mean it.

Sincerely,

Buddy

Buddy visited Nashville again and took me to lunch one day. He showed me a song he had co-written with Dave Pomeranz. I didn't like one line and told him so. "Maybe she'll lay her head on my shoulder" violated one of the rules Buddy taught in his class. Soon after that conversation, Barry Manilow made that song ("The Old Songs") a big hit. I concluded that anyone can learn to write songs, but very few will ever write hit songs.

Years after writing dozens of "rare songs," I took some essay writing classes and guitar lessons. I began submitting short stories and essays for publication. I collected a file of rejection letters, two of which were quite nice. The best was from a magazine publisher in Canada who sent a handwritten note that said something like this: "You're a good writer, and your story is funny. I enjoyed reading it. Unfortunately, it's not for us." I'm proud of that letter.

Here is my point: I am not a hit songwriter, novelist, published essay writer, photographer, or professional guitar player. I'm on the other end of the spectrum from Joe Walsh, but I share something in common with him: "Life's been good to me so far." I am happy that my mother taught me to be playful, and I'm pleased to have learned some forms of creative expression. I'm grateful to have experienced my father's work ethic. Mom was too easy to please, and Dad expected more than I delivered. One without the other might have immobilized me.

Daydreamers and Rule-Breakers

In most people, the brain's "working memory network" (alert state) deactivates when they sleep, and the "default network" (dreamy state) activates. The opposite happens when they are awake; that is, the default network deactivates. But in some individuals, there is less of a distinction and more continuity between night dreaming and daydreaming, according to Dr. Barry Scott Kaufman. The creative individuals are the daydreamers. Creative people, he said, have a more active default network even when awake and can use both networks at once. What that means is that daydreamers are able to use their ability to imagine in creative ways.

Songwriters are among the dawdling daydreamers who "didn't apply themselves" in school and got into trouble for not following the rules. Researchers have discovered that daydreaming can be a productive activity. Albert Einstein was an expert daydreamer. He called daydreaming "the residue of wasted time."

Unfortunately, daydreaming is too often associated with wasting time and misbehaving in school. If all behavior is motivated, as developmental psychologists explain, then understanding why someone is more motivated to daydream than listen to a boring lecture might lead to innovative teaching strategies. Punishing children for daydreaming is ineffective. To suggest that a child is not motivated is to describe his behavior from a false premise.

The Buddha sat a lot. He spent countless hours meditating. Learning to quiet his mind became a path to his enlightenment. Gandhi did the same and led India to independence. Einstein was a committed daydreamer. Stephen Hawkings was a daydreamer who discovered important facts about our universe, like the existence and nature of black holes.

"This boy is capable of doing anything in school, but he won't pay attention."

What songwriters have said about their childhoods reveals some features of creativity that individuals with ADHD may share. Somehow, the successful songwriters managed to disregard the censors, those who would suggest that they were wasting their time chasing fool's gold. The following examples are excerpts from Paul Zollo's book, *Songwriters on Songwriting.* In his preface Zollo quotes Bob Dylan: "There's no rule."

Merle Haggard started writing songs about the same time he started getting "those bad report cards" in the fifth or sixth grade. *This boy is capable of doing anything in school, but he won't pay attention,* his teachers said of him. "They said I was looking out the window. I guess I was writing songs then…the things they were teaching me didn't seem to be very entertaining, by any means."

Gerry Goffin said that Carole King's parents were opposed to her idea of writing songs for a living. He said, "My father encouraged me, but my mother thought I was crazy. My marks in school fell down a lot." He told his mother he could do both, go to school and write songs. "Carole ended up coaching me on all my subjects one day and failed all of hers."

Asked why he chose songwriting as a career, Randy Newman said, "You know, it might be a psychological defect." When Newman was in school at UCLA, says Zollo, "he had been known to turn around and go home when he couldn't find an easy parking spot."

Jimmy Webb's father was a Baptist preacher. When he was a kid, he sat in his father's church with a science fiction book under his hymnal. His father openly called him out, asking him to come down the aisle and stand in front of the congregation. "Tell this congregation what you're reading." Jimmy Webb replied, "*Martian Chronicles.*"

Tom Petty "rejected formal music education in favor of learning from friends." In high school he started to play in bands to impress girls. John Fogerty started making up songs in the third grade while walking to school. He started his first band when he was fourteen.[15]

Vincent Van Gogh had difficulty managing his personal life and his relationships, but he honored his passion and produced a timeless painting almost weekly. J.K. Rowling once said that she wrote the Harry Potter books because she was disorganized and unsuccessful in her attempts to be a teacher or a clerical worker.

So, what do we make of all this? It is conceivable that many of these creative people had brains wired like yours. What do you want to do with it? If you have never participated in an exercise to identify your values, I would suggest that you find a life coach to help you answer the question, "What do I want to do with my life?" Then ask yourself if you are engaging daily in activities that are related to those values. If not, you might need some coaching to create your blueprint for actualizing your dreams.

KEY POINTS TO PONDER:

- Your ADHD brain may be wired for creativity.

- What songwriters have said about their childhoods reveals some features of creativity that individuals with ADHD may share.

- You might need some coaching to actualize your creative potential.

QUESTIONS FOR REFLECTION:

- If you think you are not creative, how do you know that?

- When you were bored in the classroom, did you ever doodle or daydream? Were you creating from your imagination?

- Have you ever thought that you were not creative because you never earned income or received recognition for your creations?

Chapter Seven

ADHD Is Funny... And It's Not

You may often laugh with friends and family about your attention challenges. At other times, you may feel embarrassed and vulnerable when your inattention and impulsivity are exposed. You have to accept that some people will not understand you. Everyone doesn't have to understand you in order for you to live well. It is nice when people understand you, but only *necessary* in your closest relationships. If the relationship is important to you, you may wish to educate that person about where the line is between funny and not funny. Derision is unacceptable in a committed relationship.

In this chapter we will turn the lights up on what is funny about ADHD and what is not. First, consider your experiences with both the joy and pain of living with ADHD:

- Being self-effacing puts others at ease.

- Being improvisational with humor brings joy to life.

- Being uninhibited can help others lighten up.

- Being uninhibited can get you and others into trouble.

- Being the brunt of someone's joke is hurtful.

- Being invisible (except for your symptoms) makes you feel disrespected.

A mindless ADHD misstep, and other people's reactions to it, can trigger old memories embedded in your brain. Sometimes a string of similar experiences—along with other people's reactions to them and the old feelings associated with them—become an invisible part of the present situation. When you are highly aroused, an independent observer might see your response to the present situation as "an overreaction." But your reaction is normal, considered within the light of both the present and the past, and it need not be a problem, as long as you are aware that your reaction is about much more than what is in front of you right now. Being mindful that your brain works that way can help you differentiate the present and the past.

Here's an example to clarify what I mean: One evening when my adult daughter was visiting and talking mostly to my wife, I was standing nearby, folding laundry and halfway tuned in to their conversation. Something they were talking about grabbed my attention, and I asked a question. They looked at each other and began to laugh. My daughter explained, "If you had been listening, you wouldn't have asked that question." I knew she wasn't bothered by my inattention, but an immediate feeling of shame rose within me. Like an instant replay, I recalled an event in my childhood when my parents and older brother exploded in laughter at me in public. I was preschool age, sitting in a booth at a small roadside café with my family, snuggled against the left side of my mother, when my elbow brushed against the odd texture of her left breast. I had never seen or felt a bra before. Touching her breast with my index finger, I asked, "What's that?" The outburst of laughter from my parents and brother drew the attention of the other diners. The spotlight was hot, and I felt deeply embarrassed. When the laughter subsided, my parents told me I should never do that. I was supposed to know better.

I shifted my attention back from this memory to the present moment, and the task of folding laundry. I smiled at my wife and daughter, whose laughter had only triggered feelings from past experiences. I smiled at these two women who know me well and love me. They meant no harm, and I knew it.

Often, people say hurtful things with the best of intentions. One of my closest friends frequently initiated activities with me and went out of his way to connect. At one time, after he thought I was becoming more forgetful, he began saying repeatedly, "You really *are* ADD!" I knew he meant no harm. But in time, the recurring observation began to annoy me. He repeated it in an email message once when I was not recalling recent information he had sent. I replied that it was not necessary for him to keep reminding me of my attention disorder. "I'm well aware of it," I wrote, "and there is a painful history associated with it." He apologized immediately: "You know I would never intentionally hurt you. I've just seen you laugh at yourself so often that it never occurred to me that you could be sensitive about the ADHD." I understood and assured him that he had no way of knowing until I told him. Soon afterward, I discovered that the messages I had been "forgetting" were ones he had been sending to an old email address that I had stopped using years before. I never saw any of the messages he assumed I was forgetting! I was delighted to tell him that *he* was forgetting my current email address!

Amusing ADHD stories abound. I hear them often in my ADHD support group, where it is safe for us to laugh at ourselves. Everyone in the room has ADHD. Who could not find the humor in our episodes of inattention? Looking for my phone while talking on it is always funny!

Here's how an almost perfectly planned camping trip went awry decades ago. My wife and I were traveling through North Carolina and stopped for a daytime visit with her brother and his family. For this vacation we were alternating between camping with our new tent and staying in hotels. Our plan for the evening was to go to a nearby campground where we would sleep and then drive on to our next destination. Around mid-day, I excused myself to drive the short distance to a state park's campground to get the early bird's pick of the best campsite. The park did not take reservations for campers. First come, first served was the deal. My brother-in-law thought I was being resourceful to pitch our tent in the best spot available—early in the afternoon—and return to his house for dinner.

We visited late into evening before departing for our campsite for the first opportunity to use our new tent. Arriving at the campground at 10:30 pm, my headlights illuminated the locked gates of the campground and the sign that I didn't notice earlier in the day: "PARK CLOSES AT 10 PM." We decided not to return to my bother-in-law's home and wake his family to ask for a night in their guest room. It would embarrass us and inconvenience them. We checked into a hotel and never told them that our new tent went camping without us that night. That story makes people laugh.

But there are times when I cannot laugh about ADHD, especially when the person characterizing me misunderstands the disorder. Some jokes are not funny. I don't laugh at jokes that are racist or sexist, and I don't like jokes about aging. Uninformed remarks about your ADHD will likely offend you. They bring up painful memories from a lifetime of judgment, criticism, and self-criticism, in which you or others may have said about you:

- You're a troublemaker.

- You don't apply yourself.

- You're smarter than you act.

- You don't care.

- You're an underachiever.

- You are lazy.

- You waste time.

- You don't think before you act.

- You would lose your head if it wasn't attached.

- You're the absent-minded professor.

No one has to tell you that being bullied, teased, fired from a job, left by a relationship partner, or laughed at creates a "file" of painful memories in your brain's cerebral cortex. There is nothing funny about those memories. They make it difficult for you to hear uninformed jokes about ADHD. You may laugh at times when others joke about it, but not always. I once passed out copies of a cartoon from *The New Yorker* magazine to participants in one of my early ADHD support group meetings. The cartoon depicted an ADHD support group and displayed—in bubbles above the group members—what each individual was thinking. Participants in the cartoon were thinking about all sorts of things and nothing at all about the meeting. To my surprise, no one in the group laughed at it. And then I realized there was nothing extraordinary in seeing ourselves portrayed as we are.

Many of the jokes about ADHD are not for you, but for people who don't actually see you. The people laughing at you might not make jokes about others with more visible disabilities. They probably wouldn't tell wheelchair jokes.

> Long before surgery corrected my distance vision, an insensitive acquaintance joked, in front of company, that my eyeglasses looked like the thick glass of a soft drink bottle. All I said in response was: "My vision problem is not funny to me." I feel the same about my brain difference.

Those of us in the ADHD family have some responsibility to educate others. Otherwise, we cannot blame the public for what they can't see. If they don't see the disability as a disability, they cannot imagine our private experiences and emotional pain. They won't see our difficulties in relationships, and they won't feel the pain of our partners who love us, yet who are negatively affected by our symptoms. They won't know how we feel when others judge our missteps, and when we judge ourselves.

But we *can* laugh with those who understand and respect us. In the video *ADD and Loving It*, produced by Rick and Ava Green, Patrick McKenna debunks popular myths about the disorder and explains it in a way that is both informative and funny. His premise is that if you accept it for what it is and what it is not, and if you are unafraid to be yourself, then you can laugh about it. You can enjoy your spirited nature and share your joy with others.

What is the difference between those times when we experience joy in laughter and times when laughter brings pain and humiliation? What matters most, it seems, is whether the attempts at humor separate us or connect us. Making someone the target of a prank separates the victim from peers. Real humor, the kind that does not victimize, relieves tension and connects us. Have you noticed how you recall painful experiences differently when you use your own pain to make *others* laugh? Comedians do it all the time.

I remember two high school classmates who used different means of eliciting laughter from other students. One was self-effacing, exposing his own vulnerabilities, while the other turned his spotlight on vulnerable peers. I believe that the latter thought he was creating an atmosphere of lightness when he said funny and hurtful things. He pointed out odd haircuts, bad acne, out-of-style clothes, social awkwardness, bad breath, and clumsiness. Students often laughed, and I suspect it was because of an internal conflict: their discomfort in remaining silent, and their fear of being the next victim.

Shamefully, I sometimes laughed for those reasons. But once *I* became a target, I woke up from mindless tolerance and felt compassion for other victims. In retrospect, I don't believe the perpetrator intended harm. I suspect he was uncomfortable socially except when he was shining his spotlight on others, and it was easy to do so with students who were different from the majority.

> Experts on bullying say that the majority of "non-bullies" — those bystanders who don't like bullying, but usually don't intervene—may have the best opportunity to make a difference in schools. That silent majority has the collective power to create an atmosphere of inclusion, and an intolerance of bullying. The third-party observer could have the back of a neurologically different student by saying to the bully, "Hey, we don't do that here." Being in the majority, the speaker would not be alone in taking this position.

To illustrate what self-effacing humor can do for us, let me introduce you to Eric. Eric is remarkably resourceful and creative with strategies and tools for living well with ADHD. He was glad to share his stories because of his successes in recent years. As severe as his ADHD can be, the quality of his life improved when he began to learn what was unique about his ADHD brain. His mishaps represent a small part of an otherwise normal and happy life. He has been successful in multiple careers and is a respected husband and father. Here are some old Eric stories—delivered in his own, un-edited words—with his permission:

Took a trip to Boston to meet with my biggest client. Left my suitcase on the front porch of my house. Didn't realize that I *didn't have luggage until I waited at the baggage claim in Boston, and then went to file a lost suitcase claim when I realized I had never checked it. I had to go to Walmart at 1 a.m. to purchase clothes for an important business meeting. Left my wallet in a cab in NYC on the last day of a three-day business trip. I had checked out of a hotel, taken a cab to a meeting at "Reader's Digest" (had my luggage with me) and left my wallet in the cab. I realized it at about 2 p.m., when I left the meeting (had a flight at 4:30) and went to hail a cab to the airport. So I found my receipt, called the cab company who tracked down the driver. He was getting off his shift at 3 p.m. on the lower east side. I had no money. Borrowed cash from my client, took a taxi. The traffic was so bad, and I had to get there right at 3 o'clock. So I walked (ran) the last ten blocks and got there totally out of breath. The guy was there and had my wallet with all my cash in it. I gave him $50 as a thank you. Missed my flight, but without a wallet, couldn't have gotten on anyway.*

"I'm that fool."

Travel is the hardest. I've gone to the airport on the wrong day, have booked tickets for the wrong day. I have left my iPad on a train (never recovered), iPhone on planes (three times and always got it back, although it cost me Fed Ex, etc). Left prescription sunglasses in airport bathrooms (never got them). Have left about half my wardrobe in hotel rooms (scarf, winter coat, ties, shoes). Left $500 cash hidden in a drawer at a hotel in Chattanooga. My kids found it during the final "dummy check." Recently left $900 cash under the floor mat of a rental car. I returned it at 6 a.m. at the Charleston airport. Remembered it at 7:15 and raced back. And sure enough, they had just found it and brought it to me. As I was walking up to the counter, I overheard the rental car guy say to the desk clerk, "Who the hell leaves $900 cash in a car…what a fool." I said, "I'm that fool!" He looked a little embarrassed.

I flew home one time and had my wife pick me up, only to realize when I got home that my car was at the airport parking lot.

The first time my wife went to meet my parents, on the way back to the airport (we left late, my fault, lost track of time), we hit bad traffic. I drove the last 15 miles on the shoulder, racing to the airport. My wife was sure we would not make it, but I said, "Follow me" and I basically bullied our way through the ticket counter, through security, and ran up to the gate where they opened the ramp door and let us on. We slumped into our seats, completely out of breath, and as the plane pulled away from the gate, I reached in my pocket where I had the keys to my parents' car. I had no idea if they had spare keys. (They did.) Dawn married me after that!

On a particularly bad day (1986) I locked my keys in my car three times - honest. Fortunately, it was an old car, and I was pretty handy with a hanger. My wife is never surprised when we get a phone call, and it starts, "Is Eric Wyse there? She says, "Yeah, what did he lose this time and where did you find it?"

The first time my wife and I flew to Chicago to visit my sister, we flew into Midway — Southwest Airlines. We got in line to get the rental and someone tried to steal my wife's wallet out of her purse. I was so distracted by it (they didn't get it), I got the rental car, we drove away and were about 60 miles from the airport when I realized that we never picked up our luggage.

This is my life.

This may be your life too. Acceptance helps Eric laugh when telling these stories, and he expects others to enjoy laughing with him. As resourceful and clever as he is, Eric would be the first to tell you that living perfectly with ADHD is an unrealistic goal, and that perfectionism can actually slow us down. He told our support group one evening that he learned an important lesson from a life coach. The lesson initially was specific to his graduate school work, but it became a metaphor that had larger implications. Eric had returned to school at age fifty to get a graduate degree. He was having points deducted on papers that he was turning in late. He wanted his papers to be perfectly written, no matter that his grades suffered from the perfectionism. He lost more points turning the papers in late than he would have lost turning imperfect papers in on time. His life coach told him, "Eighty percent on time is better than 100 percent late." Already creative and resourceful, he learned to live more easily with his ADHD by recognizing that his perfectionism was an obstruction to his goals. Living well with ADHD meant accepting imperfection and embracing flexibility. In many situations, Eric's perfectionism is a strength that serves him well. But in his academic work, the same quality was a weakness that was inhibiting his efforts.

"No one is good at everything," says Dr. Ari Tuckman, in his book *More Attention and Less Deficit: Success Strategies for Adults with ADHD.* "Everyone else has to work to achieve success despite their weaknesses; they may just be different weaknesses…"

> When you get excessively focused on any task, you risk getting stuck trying to perfect something, which can obscure the big picture. The big picture comes into focus when you shift back into a state of open awareness, just like shifting your visual attention from this book to your back yard. In effect, Eric's life coach helped him return to open awareness, where he could see from a wider angle, so to speak.

If you are going to live well with ADHD, you must be willing to start where you are, accept your brain as it is, and accept your history as it was. If you can do that, and laugh with no loss of respect for yourself, you can live well.

Remember what Ben (played by Luke Wilson) said to Meredith (played by Sarah Jessica Parker) in the movie, *The Family Stone:* "Here's the thing, Meredith. You have a freak flag…you just don't fly it."

Don't be afraid to be you. Fly your freak flag! Laugh at yourself, and forgive those who laugh at you from ignorance. It would be nice if they could understand you, but don't think for a moment that they must in order for you to achieve your goals. You owe it to yourself, and to your ADHD peers, to let your light shine. And we have an obligation to future generations to educate the public about our neurological differences. ADHD is visible only in its effects, but invisible at its source.

KEY POINTS TO PONDER:

- Adults with ADHD have some responsibility to educate others. If others don't understand ADHD, they cannot imagine your private emotional experiences.

- The difference between experiencing humor as joy or humiliation depends on whether attempts at humor separate us or connect us.

- Acceptance means starting where you are.

- If you can accept how your brain is wired and laugh with no loss of self-respect, then you can live well with your ADHD.

QUESTIONS FOR REFLECTION:

- Have others made jokes about your ADHD? What is the difference between those times when you find them funny and the times when your feelings are hurt?

- Do you recall a time when you felt diminished by someone's joke?

- Are there any specific painful events in your history that have been triggered by insensitive jokes?

- What can you do when you feel someone is making fun of you because of your ADHD symptoms?

- In what ways have you let your freak flag fly? When is the last time you flew it?

79

Chapter Eight

Success Stories

Do you often feel like you are an underachiever, no matter what you have accomplished? Have you had many big ideas and failed to sustain your effort enough to actualize them? Have you fallen so far short of your vision that you feel you no longer have a vision? If not for the inspiration of many successful people with ADHD whom I've known, I might never have started writing this book. Throughout my life, I started many tasks and projects that I never completed.

Don't measure success by financial gain, but by how effectively you are living a life that you value. One of the most brilliant and interesting young men I know learned how to live happily and productively with less material wealth than most people in this country could survive on. Spencer grows affordable organic produce for low-income families who, otherwise, could not afford nutritious food, and for restaurants whose purchases support the program. And as you might imagine, he grows much of his own food. He has no interest in television and time-wasting gadgets that could compromise living mindfully. His mindfulness practice is mostly in real time, in his daily life, where it counts most.

In this chapter, I describe the lives and achievements of other interesting men and women who learned to live well with their ADHD.

Running to Catch Up

Corinne is an entrepreneur and an artist. She owns her own hair salon and paints with oils. Petite and spirited, she talks nonstop while grooming me. Thanks to medication, she also listens when I explain how I want my hair cut. I like her art, and so I asked if she earns income from it. She told me she gives away most of it because she worries that making a vocation of her art might take the joy out of it.

Corinne was diagnosed with ADHD the same day that her son was. After diagnosing Jeff at age twelve, and prescribing stimulant medication for him, his physician turned to Corinne and asked, "So when are you going to treat *your* ADHD?" She began taking the same medication as her son. She had a unique opportunity to observe the effects of medication, having her own experience and observing her son's.

Corinne did not want Jeff to give too much attention to his medicine. She told him to take it and forget about it, and she kept it secret from his teachers. She wanted him to focus on learning and living, rather than on his medicine. Dexedrine would level the playing field for him, allowing him an opportunity to "run to catch up," as she put it. He had gotten behind in school.

Jeff had been evaluated by a psychologist who thought that his only problem was poor parenting. The psychologist told Corinne, "One day he will run all over you." That day never came. A twice-divorced, strong, and independent woman, Corinne knew better and disregarded the prediction.

"I knew it wasn't true," she said. She told Jeff that he could not deceive her because she knew all the tricks, having grown up with the same kind of brain. He would not be able to convince her that he lacked competence. This budding teen, who was certain to run all over her, now has a divinity degree and is an ordained minister.

When Corinne first took the same medicine that Jeff's physician prescribed for him, she felt as if someone suddenly turned the lights on. Despite her intelligence and resourcefulness, teachers and family members didn't see her as she saw herself. "They acted like I just didn't know anything," she told me. "I couldn't do anything right. I wouldn't listen." After beginning treatment, her family continued their misperceptions of her.

One day she gave her brother some unsolicited advice regarding his computer. He was certain she knew nothing about computers and told her so. He insisted that his new modem was not compatible with his computer. She told him he was wrong and explained why he was failing to connect it correctly. "You don't know anything about computers," he told her. But he tried what she suggested and it worked. Still, he thought she had made a lucky guess and continued to believe that she knew nothing about computer hardware. Then she built a computer for her mother, after having experimented with taking motherboards apart and building new computers from old parts. When her brother asked their mom where she got her new computer, she replied, "Corinne built it." He knew better. "Corinne could not have built that computer," he told his mother.

In time, her brother came to respect her skills and even consulted her when he had problems with his own computers. His change was gradual, as he observed her skills and resourcefulness over time, but hers was a swift transformation.

Like most of us on the ADHD spectrum, Corinne was not an easy adolescent to parent. "I self-medicated when I was young," she told me. At the time, she did not know why she was so drawn to alcohol and drugs. She was aware that her experience was different from most of her peers. She could sit still and focus when high. But now she has no desire at all to use any illicit drug, and she seldom drinks. "I don't need it to enjoy life," she said. She would rather jump out of a plane, paint with oils, or have a stimulating conversation. She taught Jeff to find stimulation in becoming resourceful and enjoying learning. When he was a child in school, she would not answer his academic questions directly. Instead, she would answer his questions with questions of her own, and then help him learn how to find answers. She believes that schools too often teach children to hate school by mostly teaching facts. She preferred teaching Jeff to love learning.

One of her salon clients disclosed to her that her son believed he had ADHD and wanted to take medicine for it. Opposed to medication in general, and ambivalent about whether ADHD was real, this mom had asked her son, "What do you see differently from what I see?" Corinne challenged her: "How can he know what you see? You may as well ask what he can see with his eyes closed." She asked the mother if she preferred that her son not see as well as he could. Why would he want to keep the lights off when he could turn them on? To another mom who was concerned that medicine was not helping her child, Corinne told her to be patient. She explained that, with medicine, her own child was able to "run to catch up." But he still had to do the work to catch up. Jeff was given a chance to run, and he caught up. In fact, he passed many of his peers.

If It Ain't Broke, Break It!

My friend Jim is a life coach specializing in career transitions. One evening he told me that an old college friend was coming to town and thought I should invite him to address my support group. A retired CEO and president of a large company, and an overachiever with ADHD, Dennis would inspire participants in the support group.

I entered the room where my group meets twice monthly and saw an old familiar face. *No way*, I thought! This man had hired me more than forty years earlier into my first full-time job, long before either of us was diagnosed with ADHD. I remembered him as one of the friendliest people in management. A tall man—his former blond hair mostly gray now, and his blue eyes still smiling—Dennis seemed too approachable to be a CEO. He was not the stereotype.

He spoke to about twenty of us that evening. Here's what he told us: When he was a CEO, he kept his goals on a 3" x 5" index card that he carried in his shirt pocket. His secretary would type and laminate the card. The lamination was to prevent him from erasing and re-writing the objectives. One of his companies had 1,700 employees, and he met with all of them in small groups in each of his first two years there. He told them that they knew their jobs better than he could ever know them, and that they probably were smarter than he was because he barely got through high school and college, and had poor grades. He promised to try to implement any ideas they had for improving the company. Their contributions made the company better, he said.

A year after Dennis visited my support group, he agreed to let me interview him by phone. I wanted first to know how he was diagnosed.

While his first daughter had made almost all A's in school, his second daughter struggled. He took her to a child development specialist, who diagnosed her ADHD. During the meeting, Dennis found himself playing a game in his head that he and his daughter often played while he drove her to school. They would imagine characteristics of drivers of interesting cars that they passed on the road. While the therapist was interviewing his daughter, Dennis was looking out the window at a yellow Chevrolet Corvette in the parking lot. He was imagining the owner's occupation and personal features when the therapist turned toward him—interrupting his daydreaming—and diagnosed *him* in that same interview. He has been taking stimulant medication daily since then.

I think you've got the wrong guy.

"I barely finished high school and barely finished college," Dennis told me. When his employers promoted him up the ranks over the years, he protested that they were making a mistake. "I think you've got the wrong guy," he would say, "I'm too disorganized." But with each promotion, his employer would dismiss Dennis' concerns and assure him he knew what he was looking for. For years Dennis was afraid that someone, somewhere along the way, would ask for his college transcripts, and he would be exposed.

Being an academic underachiever gave him some advantages as a CEO. He sincerely believed that the most important sources of knowledge in a company were its employees. They were the experts in their jobs. They knew their work environments. He had the wisdom to empower them, and empowering came naturally to him. But he knew that he needed their expertise, their ideas, and their commitment. Collectively, they could change the culture of their company, and they did.

He recalled his first general managerial position, where he would show up on different shifts to meet his employees and learn about their jobs and their families. One evening he met Ricky, an employee who had an idea for solving a problem that had plagued the company for years. Dennis promised to get him an audience with the company's fifteen engineers. He could not promise any result, but he could promise a meeting. The engineers responded to Ricky's suggestion with blank faces that Dennis translated as, "Why did we never think of that?" Ricky was not an engineer, and yet he solved an engineering problem.

Dennis sometimes speaks to groups of executives. He tells them to trust their instincts: "There is something wrong with how this person interacts with customers…something is not working quite right here." (There is evidence that adults with ADHD may have reason to trust their instincts, as they are more attuned to the big picture and less encumbered with the details.)

In one company, where he was CEO of U.S. operations, Dennis reserved about $1.3 million for $1,000 incentive payments to a large number of employees who, at the time, were not on an incentive plan. The CEO of international operations disagreed with the idea, believing that a one-time bonus was not worth the risk of spending that much. "Listen to me carefully," he told Dennis, "I wouldn't do that if I were you." Dennis told his wife that evening that he might be losing his job because he had argued with his boss and then sent out $1.3 million in checks to his employees. The employees were shocked and grateful, and the company continued to grow.

Dennis told me his philosophy was, "If it ain't broke, break it." He explained that managers should not be afraid to make big changes, especially when the changes serve the people who keep the company running. Dennis thrived on the strengths of his ADHD brain; it helped him be a "people person" who sees the big picture. He received hundreds of thank you notes from those who received the bonus checks. The company went from breaking even to breaking through the roof, and Dennis wanted to reward those who made it happen.

Encouragement Changes Lives

When I first met Troy, he was a hyperactive, quick-witted, skinny teenager who could get his brown hair out of his eyes by swinging his head upward and to the right. This freckle-faced teenager talked so fast, I had to slow him down so I could comprehend what he was telling me. He was bored to tears in his first high school, an academic magnet in the public school system. He lobbied his parents to transfer him to an arts magnet, and he transferred schools at the beginning of his sophomore year. A talented guitar player, Troy liked the arts magnet school. He admitted that he didn't have to do much work there.

Troy was a comic who always made me laugh. He liked to smoke marijuana on occasion. Although he was not a serious abuser, and was not particularly interested in alcohol or drugs, I worried that he could compromise his potential. He was open to my challenges and yet smart enough to learn more by observing peers in his adolescent world.

One night, Troy had a date with a girl who lived in an affluent suburb. They went to a party in her neighborhood. He got bored quickly, as everyone seemed interested in little else but drinking. His date got drunk, and Troy was disgusted. He insisted on leaving early and was driving her home when a policeman, who had been monitoring the party from down the street, pulled him over. Troy was not one to clean out his car often. He had an empty beer can on the floorboard in the back and a bottle of vodka that had been opened. He was cited for underage possession of alcohol, lost his driving privileges for six months, and had to work in community service while on probation. The experience woke him from the typical adolescent delusion of invincibility and illuminated real-life risks of mindlessness.

Troy's younger sister was an achiever and a rule follower. Although Troy was not an in-your-face defiant kid, he did not walk a straight line and was not as easy for his parents. He was definitely not a kid with oppositional defiant disorder, a common problem for adolescents who have hyperactive and impulsive features. Troy just had a mild aversion to imposition. He was just a friendly comedian who was uncensored and self-directed.

When I caught up with Troy for this interview, he had published a paper in a scientific journal, had begun writing his dissertation for a doctorate in clinical psychology, had written a chapter in a book on ADHD, and was in the middle of planning his wedding. He made all A's from the beginning of undergraduate school through his PhD program at a major university. He told me he had started taking medication consistently only after he started college. He took it inconsistently in high school "for social reasons." He continues to take medication daily. He credited medication, and one encouraging teacher, for his ability to live well with ADHD.

"Criticism makes kids want to give up."

Troy had liked school, he said, until his first magnet school experience, where he struggled all through the ninth grade. It was the only time he had performed poorly in school, he said. He had never had so much homework. The academic magnet was difficult, he said, and his teachers thought of him as a behavior problem. "They made me feel bad about myself," he said. He acknowledged *looking like* a behavior problem. He always felt overwhelming guilt for his poor performance after procrastinating and prioritizing his video games over studying. He would berate himself. "That is why one encouraging teacher can make a difference," he told me. "Criticism makes kids want to give up."

In his senior year, when he was beginning to think about college, an English teacher saw Troy's potential and encouraged him. She not only knew how to teach, she knew how to connect with kids, he said. He attributes his eventual success to his English teacher's encouragement, to stimulant medication, and to learning how to forgive himself for procrastinating—instead of becoming more obstructed by guilt. "I am an advocate for medicine," he told me. And he believes in unconditional positive regard.

Riding the Waves

Chuck resembles a picture of his Italian grandmother. Her image is on the label of the tomato sauce (her recipe) that he sells at one of his restaurants. He took me upstairs in one of his places of business for our interview. The business in this building, one he shares with his girlfriend, was a patchwork of holistic services, literature about healthy living, and a menu of wholesome vegetarian and vegan items.

Chuck moved from an Italian neighborhood in upstate New York to Nashville, where he now owns three successful restaurants. Family pictures decorate the walls in one of his restaurants. I had met him years earlier in my ADHD support group.

Before interviewing him, I checked him out online and found several YouTube videos. In one, he was interviewed by a local television news reporter who was interested in his rooftop garden. Chuck had run out of space to grow fresh vegetables and herbs for his restaurants when he was replacing a roof. Looking at the flat rooftop, he realized the potential for more garden space there and installed a tower gardening system. Chuck is an idea person, a divergent problem solver, who is unafraid to trust his instincts.

"I use coffee as medication," Chuck told me. "I don't take medicine anymore. I tried it begrudgingly twice because of coaxing by my ex-wife. I was way too sensitive to it because it didn't coincide with my biorhythms, my waves of high performance and down times." He spoke of having learned to "ride the waves." His levels of energy and attentiveness are variable. On those occasions when energy is high, he rides that wave by having high expectations and using the energy to accomplish much work. When his energy is low, he has learned not to berate himself, and he relaxes into a slower pace with lowered expectations. Acceptance of both states, and recognizing the impermanence of either, has helped him keep moving forward.

"I remember a young man in the support group lamenting, 'If only my boss would let me come to work at 3 a.m.' I totally get that!" Chuck said. "Ride the wave, the biorhythm, the mood. I recognized a long time ago this almost manic wave of inspiration. Sometimes it lasted for a month, at other times a day or two. And the low parts were not so low when I knew I'd have a high again. I still got a lot done during the low times, but it felt more like going through the motions than inspired living."

There is a downside to riding the wave, he said. "It's fine for me to say that I go with my mood and that I ride the wave, but it affects everybody around me. Others don't necessarily like riding someone else's waves," he told me. "I'm very aware that it's not how the rest of the world operates. Not everyone is in the mood for a bike ride late at night." He worries about how his ADHD affects his family, especially his kids: "It creates an unnecessary burden on them because of my thoughtlessness and lack of timeliness."

Chuck wishes to contribute to the success of others with ADHD. He advocates getting a good night's sleep. He makes a list before going to bed at night. "Even if I don't use it the next day, I need to 'put it somewhere.' I don't need to be trying to remember things at bedtime and keeping my mind racing as a result." He believes in having a mindful diet, as he has observed that his energy level is "ultra sensitive to sugar and heavy foods."

He said he knows well how low self-esteem comes about. "I had to rethink my whole life, playing back scenarios in my head from my childhood through school, recalling the frustration of parents and teachers…and mostly of myself."

"Know thyself."

Chuck feels fortunate to be self-employed. "I'm psychologically unemployable," he told me. "How can someone with ADHD hold a job?" He said he learned that "dysfunction can lead to great achievement." He knew he had to figure out how to be self-employed. "If you ask my ex-wife, I'm positive she'd tell you that my ADHD, and being self-employed, scared the shit out of her. I don't blame her. I was an untested commodity and starting a restaurant from scratch. I was scared too, but I was willing to take risks. Our backgrounds were different. Everyone in her family had jobs. My parents, grandparents, uncles, and cousins were all self-employed."

"Know thyself," Chuck said. "Not knowing I had ADHD as a young man destroyed me and my first marriage, and it was unfair to her. I did not know who I was or what was to come. I was angry and stupid, but mostly scared, and I didn't even know why. My poor ex-wife... I've apologized several times. Maybe it's just being young, but the ADHD exacerbated my anxiety and lack of direction. Now I feel like I've come a long way, but in some respects, I feel like I'm fifteen years behind in my career and potential."

Chuck's perception of being behind and underachieving is part of what drives him toward excellence. His restaurants get frequent recognition for the quality of their food and service, and he is recognized as a successful entrepreneur in a competitive urban environment. He refuses to let his ADHD obstruct him. And his resourcefulness is extraordinary. After being inconvenienced by frequent loss of keys, he determined that it would be cost-effective to purchase a key-making machine. Now, whenever he has a new key, he immediately makes several copies of it and keeps the labeled copies in a safe place.

Doing and Being

Connie and Sheila are business partners as well as relationship partners. They share a real estate brokerage business, own investment properties, host a podcast, and successfully navigate a relationship that embraces Connie's ADHD and Shelia's OCD. Their differences created some problems before Connie's ADHD diagnosis. Sheila willingly took on the task of learning about ADHD and how to support Connie, and how to partner effectively with Connie's attention management challenges. Shelia admires Connie's special strengths, which she attributes to her ADHD brain. Connie can look at a property, envision what a renovation will look like, and then make it happen. She plunges straight ahead. Sheila, on the other hand, is the organized partner who can keep a steady pace.

She can keep Connie grounded, and Connie can fire up Shelia's excitement. Each partner's way of operating in the world makes sense to the other because of their efforts to understand and accept each other unconditionally.

They attended my ADHD couple's workshop, and Sheila frequently accompanied Connie to the ADHD support group. While participation in the support group normally is exclusively for the ADHD individual only, Sheila's participation helped Connie and the group. Their commitment to competent partnering became an inspiring model for others in the group who are in long-term relationships.

Connie wrote a book about living consciously. Her writing project began as an effort to help people understand grief. Through the process of writing, Connie learned something about herself: (1) She had not truly grieved her brother's death, and (2) she had a problem with telling people what they should do. She said writing her book became as much a learning experience for her as for her readers. She discovered that she had more to learn about grieving before she could inform others. Her story began with the loss of her brother, a homicide victim whose murder was never solved.

Connie told me that she set out to write a book that would instruct and inspire people who were grieving. After all, she had experience. But writing would unravel her unfinished business: the protracted pain of wishing to know what happened to her brother; her strong will to find some kind of resolution; and the resentment that she managed to keep at bay with her exceptional drive and work ethic. She told me she could run, but she could not be still. While writing daily, she learned to be still, to be with her loss instead of trying to run past it. She learned that being with it was the essence of grieving. Doing was easy for her; being was a greater challenge. She discovered that she could not begin to let go while holding on.

With loving support from her friends and her partner, Connie began to accept her loss and the unsolved murder mystery. She learned acceptance and compassion through studying and practicing meditation. Coincidentally, the meditation practice enhanced her ability to activate, manage her attention, and sustain her effort.

She read about ADHD, and observed how it affected her daily functioning and her relationship. She learned to let go of self-criticism, and to be more compassionate toward herself. What helped with the unfinished grieving also helped her to accept her ADHD brain and live well with it. She didn't have to prove her worth. She didn't have to be perfect. She could allow someone to do for her what she would do for others. Perhaps most important to her, forgiving her brother's killer didn't have to mean abandoning her brother. In fact, she would begin to honor her brother's life by living her own, as he would have wished for her.

KEY POINTS TO PONDER:

- Many people with ADHD are living successful, enriching lives—often because of their ADHD. There is no reason why you can't too.

- The best way to measure your success in life is by asking yourself: Am I living the life I want to live? Am I achieving my goals?

- There is evidence that adults with ADHD may have good reason to trust their instincts. They are more attuned to the big picture and less encumbered by all the little pieces.

- Be mindful of how your ADHD-related behavior affects others, but try to forgive yourself and refrain from excessive, counter-productive self-criticism.

QUESTIONS FOR REFLECTION:

- Do you identify with any of the individuals described in this chapter? In what way are you like one or more of them?

- Do you have a vision for something you wish to achieve in your life? After reading this chapter, what is the probability that you can achieve it?

- Do you feel your ADHD sometimes gives you an advantage in life? If so, how?

- What story inspired you the most? What will you do with this inspiration?

Chapter Nine

The Color of Life:
Living Skillfully with Your Emotions

If you are like most adults with ADHD, you probably have trouble inhibiting your actions when bathed in strong emotional arousal. You may have trouble settling down and shifting your attention away from the object of your aroused feelings. Your impulsive brain may not allow enough space between an event and your reaction to it, and you might not always respond in a skillful manner. You may be avoiding or escaping unpleasant emotions without realizing it. Your mind may be moving at such a fast pace that you don't see what it is avoiding or escaping.

Let me begin with some questions before you read on:

- Have you ever become enraged when cut off by a driver on the freeway?

- Have you been so hyper-focused on a preferred activity that you got angry when interrupted?

- Did you ever get angry so quickly that you said something regrettable and then wished you could back up and start over?

- Have you felt so overwhelmed by the many tasks facing you that you gave up and turned on the television or surfed the Internet instead of starting the tasks?

- Have you felt hopeless?

- Did you ever get so excited about something that you felt almost manic?

- Have you ever felt like you needed to rid yourself of anxiety so you could confront someone you have been avoiding, or make a cold call to someone you don't know?

- Are you a worrier?

- Did you ever worry about worrying so much, or feel anxious about becoming anxious?

No one wishes for uncomfortable feelings. But wishing not to have them will cause problems you don't want to have. A recurring desire for life to be "some other way" causes suffering. Accepting life as it is, including normal discomfort, is emotionally healthy. When the NFL's Tennessee Titans started their summer rookie camp with Heisman Trophy winner Marcus Mariota, camera crews and journalists swarmed around the young quarterback. The headline in *The Tennessean's* sports section the next morning read, "MARIOTA A LITTLE ANXIOUS". After practice, the star of the 2015 draft told *The Tennessean* reporter, "It felt good. I was a little anxious." He went on to say, "I am going to build relationships and try to enjoy this wonderful game we play." He didn't say that he hoped to get rid of anxious feelings so he could enjoy himself and play with confidence. He *felt good and was a little anxious.* I don't believe it was coincidental that he connected feeling good with feeling a little anxious. He showed this kind of emotional maturity throughout his remarkable college career at the University of Oregon.

Life events are just realities that we all must confront, even though you may have more than your share of difficult circumstances. You still have to play the game of life on its terms. It won't help to wish the rules were different, the opponent were easier, or the game would just unfold as you wish it to. You are in charge of your life, including the emotional part of it, and it is up to you to be skillful in managing how you deal with your feelings while you deal with your life circumstances. The more skillful you are in dealing with your emotional life, the more competently you can manage your life's challenges.

Accepting life on its own terms allows you to be real. Trying to avoid or escape discomfort is denying reality and avoiding life, which is the opposite of acceptance. You cannot make life conform to your ideal. Trying to do so is a prescription for discontent. You can't stop the ocean's waves by pushing back against them. And you can't stop emotional waves. You experience their impermanence when you simply observe them rising, washing over you, and subsiding. And you can count on the inevitability that other waves will follow. Life is like that.

Even pleasurable waves are impermanent, and being aware of that reality allows you to embrace joy more fully in happy times. When you accept uncomfortable and joyful feelings as equally impermanent, you can relate to the uncomfortable ones. You might think of unpleasant emotions as being like the weather in Denver. A friend there once told me, "If you don't like the weather in Denver, just wait five minutes."

Psychotherapists often speak of emotional styles, mental habits, and states of mind. However you label them, habits of the mind can be self-defeating or constructive.

In this chapter we will explore the nature of your emotional life—how your emotions influence your thoughts, and how your thoughts, in turn, fuel your emotions. We will address:

- feelings as temporary waves that rise and subside in your body

- the relationship between anxiety and inflexible thinking

- the problem of mistaking your thoughts for absolute truths

- observing your feelings and thoughts without judging them

- changing your habitual patterns of emotionally reactive thinking

- accepting life on its terms in order to live it fully

First, you must understand that emotions are an important part of living and coping. They alert you to danger, prompt you to act, and stimulate empathy. They attract you to others, and protect you from others. They have many useful functions. Fear, anger, and sadness are not abnormal.

Clients often tell me, in so many words, that they need to rid themselves of anxiety so they can act. They get it backwards. They need to act, despite their feelings and carry the anxiety with them if necessary. They do not need to let emotions run their lives. The notion that you must *resolve* or *get over* some feeling in order to act is self-defeating nonsense. To be anxious about becoming anxious, for example, is to move in the wrong direction. Trying to avoid anxious discomfort compounds it. It's like trying to think your way out of an excessive thinking problem. Good luck with that! Making comfort too high a priority is self-defeating. Making everything in life gray and predictable in order to be safe will cause you to miss all of the many colors of life.

Old notions about getting your anger *out*, so you can be free of it, assumes that there is a problem having it in. Having the capacity for angry feelings is normal. Emotional intelligence is being smart about *what to do* with your feelings, and not about *getting rid of them*. There is mounting evidence that the old idea of getting anger out, while helping you to feel better momentarily, actually contributes to *more* problems with anger, not fewer. Hitting a pillow, for example, can feel good when you are angry, but it doesn't make you any smarter about how to relate to your angry feelings when provoked.

When you are in your busy mind, where mental chatter is nonstop like white noise, you are unlikely to notice the rising and subsiding of physical sensations in your body, those temporary shifts we call feelings. Subtle shifts in your emotional state can go unnoticed, like an invisible force driving your actions. Waking up to them keeps them in their proper role wherein they protect you without taking charge of your life. But you might not know when you are trying to avoid or escape them, thereby allowing them too much influence. Mindlessness about your internal world can be as harmful as mindlessness about the external world. Fear-driven thoughts can have you believing that life is to be avoided, and that safety and comfort are more important than living. Anger-driven judgments can separate you from others. Hopelessness and despair can rob you of your vision and purpose.

Skill-based therapies with names like MBCT (mindfulness-based cognitive therapy), MBSR (mindfulness-based stress reduction), ACT (acceptance and commitment therapy) are proving to be effective medicine for anxiety and depression, and perhaps as effective as pharmaceuticals. In fact, the relapse rate appears to be lower with these therapies than with medicine alone. The working premise of mindfulness-based therapies is that the brain can change the brain. In other words, you can use your brain's amazing capacity to develop new mental habits that will effectively defeat the old habits.

Anxiety

By practicing mindfulness of your body and your emotional state, you are learning to notice the moments when your emotional state suddenly shifts into anxious discomfort. Mine just shifted a few minutes ago when I glanced at my bills and saw the mortgage statement at the top of the stack. A sinking feeling swept over me, and it subsided quickly when I simply noticed an accompanying irrational thought—that I shouldn't have to pay it now because my cash flow is limited. Like most "should" and "shouldn't" thoughts, it was a superfluous one that had no value. The feeling may arise briefly again tonight when I prepare to pay my bills. But the wave will subside again unless I reattach to the thought that I shouldn't have to pay them right now. My automatic story line just isn't true. In fact, the anxious feeling will begin to subside the moment I write the checks, and I always feel at peace when the checks are in the mail on time.

Geraldo, a young adult client whom I had not seen in two years, recently asked to resume therapy. "I've been allowing myself to feel anxious lately," he told me. He was uncomfortable when separated from his girlfriend, even for short periods. He would become anxious when she was neither sending him text messages, nor replying immediately to his. She was often just busy studying or working. I told him that his conclusion—that he was allowing himself to feel anxious—was the opposite of the truth. "The problem," I said, "is that you are *not* allowing yourself to feel anxious." He was not tolerating the mild discomfort of distance from his girlfriend, and he created more discomfort by repeatedly texting her. In its raw form, the mild discomfort was not extraordinary. But the discomfort grew when it drove his emotion-thought: "I must not be as important to her as her work." And it grew exponentially when she didn't reply promptly. The simple reality, he acknowledged, was that she was often unable to reply when at work.

Unwillingness was Geraldo's problem, not feelings. He was unwilling to feel a little unsettled, and in an effort to get settled, his brain was generating possible threats in the form of thoughts and images that he must rule out by questioning his girlfriend. That self-protecting capacity of his brain was trying to protect him from imagined loss. Do you see how important this is? He was reacting not to real loss, but only to *imagined* loss! His fear-driven story lines turned out to be the only real risks to the relationship.

"It makes no sense that I'm doing this," he said. "I trust her completely, and this is starting to annoy her." Again, I challenged him to suspend belief in what he was thinking—that it doesn't make sense. In a way of speaking, everything makes sense. We just don't always have enough pieces of the puzzle to see how the pieces form a picture. He needed to remain curious about how this mental habit developed. To say that it doesn't make sense only circumvents curiosity. He considered the influences in his family. He volunteered that his mother was always anxious when separated from him. She recently moved and now lives two hours away from him. One evening when his cell phone battery had run down, he called his mother from a friend's phone, a number that she recognized. She answered not with a hello, but with, "What's wrong?" His mother and maternal grandmother were worriers, he said, often anticipating imagined catastrophes.

A cognitive behavior therapy expert once described obsessive worry as "trying to control the future by thinking about it." When Geraldo was in high school, his mother often worried that he would have trouble fitting in with his peers because he had a physical disability. But his "disability" was not disabling him, as he would not allow it to limit his life. He did not lack courage. He always maintained that he was more adaptive than his mother about such matters. But her empathy overstated his reality, fermenting her belief that he was in denial (and it is hard to deny denial!). It made sense that a young person would resonate with his mother's anxiety, which was pronounced when he was separated from her. This was Geraldo's experience from youth to now. In effect, he was emotionally reactive to his mother's emotional reactivity. Her anxiety gave birth to his. He had developed a distorted notion about feelings—the idea that anxious discomfort is abnormal, that something must be done to escape or avoid such unacceptable feelings!

When feelings override your thoughts, you will experience a presumed threat as a real threat, calling for real action. In this case, anxious discomfort prompted the story line that Geraldo was becoming unimportant in his girlfriend's life. Whatever she was doing when away from him was more important. He began to believe that he might not be enough for her. Buying this thought, as if it were the truth, led to a bigger problem in reality. She was becoming annoyed that he had such trouble trusting her commitment to the relationship. He assured her that he trusted her. But she countered that he often looked disappointed whenever she informed him that she was going to be busy for much of the day. She wished not to feel responsible for his disappointment.

Geraldo's *thought* that he might be losing his girlfriend— which was the only real problem—was influencing him to engage in behavior that put the relationship at risk. Willingness to risk the relationship for the short-term benefit of reassurance was backward. He needed only to tolerate the mild discomfort of brief separation from her to actually decrease the risk of losing her.

The stronger the feeling of arousal, the more inflexible Geraldo's thinking became. In my meetings with him, I felt his discomfort and heard his desperation. With his help, I could see the big waves of emotion. He was experiencing the mixed emotions of love and fear, and he was determined to stop the waves of fear. Areas of his brain responsible for protecting him from harm were overwhelming him to the point that his reasoning was obstructed. His fear stimulated and reinforced negative thinking, which prompted even more emotional distress.

Practicing the skill of observing waves (feelings) non-judgmentally, and detaching from story lines (thoughts), is essential to living well with emotions. Thinking about thoughts doesn't reduce mental activity. Simply noticing them without judgment does. Observing the natural rising and subsiding of emotions will help you practice suspending belief in your story lines. Geraldo's story line was clear to me: *The wave must be stopped!*

There are good reasons for having the capacity to experience fear and anxiety. It is adaptive. Anxious arousal alerts you to react immediately and leaves no room, at the moment of your arousal, for the slower process of reasoning. Processing too slowly can get you run over by a car or fired from a job. Nothing is wrong when your brain's natural arousal system is working; it just might be working too well. Knowing that the arousal is just a healthy function gone awry can help. Sometimes it is like a big wave. You wouldn't tell the ocean that there is no reason for such a big wave. It wouldn't be true. You just might not know what the reason is, which doesn't really matter. When you make it matter, you make the wave the problem, rather than your reaction to it. A moderate degree of anxiety makes for good citizenship. It prompts us to pay our bills and taxes on time and obey the law.

The way to recover your reasoning brain, when it spikes disproportionately to the situation, is to respect it the way you might respect a guard dog for being prepared to protect you. Respect your capacity to feel and avoid real danger. Respect your brain's remarkable ability to imagine so vividly that your emotions react to your own imagery, as if the images are actual events. The capacity to anticipate real danger is adaptive. But the corresponding anxious feelings contribute to *certainty* of risk, and in the interest of your protection, your fear-driven thoughts will *overstate* danger before they will *understate* it. There is no time for uncertainty when it comes to survival, no time to understate the risk or to engage the "reasoning brain," which operates more deliberately and more slowly. The job of your brain's limbic system is to take charge and protect you; it doesn't allow time for doubt. Consequently, it is subjective and not always right. It is reacting at the speed of light and judging impulsively, rather than observing and reasoning. To those who believe your first instinct is always right, think again!

When you believe something is true only because you *feel* it is true, you can defeat yourself, as Geraldo was doing. Slowing down the wheels of emotional reactivity will help you suspend your story line and engage more of your brain so you can reason skillfully. Your gut could be right, but your emotional brain needs the reliability check of your reasoning brain. Informed by emotions, but not controlled by them, the reasoning brain can remain in charge.

Anger

Angry feelings have their place in your life. Without them you might not assert yourself when you need to, you may fail to protect yourself from being exploited, or you may even be unaware of what you need. Angry feelings can also contribute to problems if you are impulsive or mindless, or if you buy your first angry thought, the story line that your emotional brain is trying to sell. You will not have a balanced thought if your observation stops at the assumed source of your anger, the person or situation that you believe "caused" it. When you pause and take a breath, allowing enough space between an event and your response to it, you can then observe your body—the rising and subsiding sensations of anger—and you can engage (or re-engage) your reasoning brain. Cultivating that space will be a challenge for you because of the ADHD and your impulsivity. Medication is sometimes necessary to have access to that space, and meditation can help you develop it through routine practice.

If you have ADHD, chances are, your impulsive tendencies have contributed to mindless actions. Anger can narrow your perspective and lead to self-defeating, selfish, or dangerous action. When I was a young driver, mild road rage could have cost me my life, as I sought to teach bad drivers a lesson. I was inclined to show a tailgater what it felt like to have someone driving dangerously close, or I would simply raise a finger to give immediate feedback. No doubt, you have said things impulsively when angry and harmed a relationship.

It is not enough to apologize and expect your outbursts to be forgiven. The outbursts have a cumulative effect. They chip away at the foundation of a relationship. They communicate the message, "You are walking into a minefield and need to be careful not to set me off." Your intentions won't matter when your actions do harm. Arousing someone's neurological security alarm for self-serving reasons is unjust.

Your impulsive anger may reflect your brain's attempt to get settled, as your aroused mind wants the other person to feel as strongly as you feel. Then they will understand. What they *will* understand for sure is that you are unreasonable. Dr. Marshall B. Rosenberg's nonviolent communication ideas focus on creating a "respectful connection" and peaceful dialogue to discover unmet needs behind a conflict. That connection precedes strategies for resolving conflict. The way we tend to communicate in conflict, he says, creates distance rather than connection. When you can express your need, and listen with an effort to understand the other person's need, you are connecting respectfully.[16] Expecting your need to be obvious to the other person—or criticizing the other person—will create distance rather than connection.

> NVC (Nonviolent Communication) is a wonderful resource for learning "how to transform conflicts into opportunities for connection" through workshops, classes, books, and free practice groups in the U.S. and other countries. It offers many free resources including daily meditations and a free newsletter. For information about NVC go to www.nonviolentcommunication.com.

Depression and Negative Thinking

Do you sometimes feel hopeless about achieving your goals or just completing a simple task? Do you feel so overwhelmed by tasks you think should be manageable that you feel resigned to a life of disappointments? Were you misdiagnosed with depression before the ADHD diagnosis? Do you have a co-existing depression? Adults with ADHD are more than twice as likely as the general population to suffer from depression.

When ADHD co-exists with clinical depression:

- you may have lost interest in activities that you once enjoyed

- you may sleep too much or too little

- you may be too alert at night and fuzzy during the day

- you may be eating too much or too little

- you are likely to have worse than normal problems with your ADHD symptoms

- you may have more difficulty focusing and sustaining your attention

- you will likely have more problems getting started and sustaining your effort

- you may be more forgetful

- you will have more difficulty with attending to details

You might need anti-depressant medication if depression is *amplifying* your ADHD symptoms. And if depression appears to be an *effect* of the ADHD—like losing a job because of being chronically late, having relationship problems due to inattention and misperceptions, underachieving because you are in an occupational mismatch, getting divorced because your partner felt disregarded or could no longer tolerate the chaos—the ADHD may be contributing to depression. In that case, your doctor may elect to treat the ADHD first. Such details of your experience are important for your physician to get from you in order to prescribe the right medicine. He will need your help to know how to prioritize what he is treating.

If the ADHD is the *primary* problem, you may have a track record of failed attempts to achieve a goal. You may have postponed action toward a life goal because you didn't feel ready or deserving to give your best effort to something you wanted to do. Or you may have chosen not to pursue something you wanted, in order to avoid failing. I'm not sure what explains the difference between the avoiders and the resilient, but it might inform us to study the latter and try to replicate what they do. They often employ some form of picking themselves up and starting over.

> There was a song about this in a 1936 movie, *Swing Time*, starring Fred Astaire and Ginger Rogers. The lyric to "Pick Myself Up" was written by Dorothy Fields (1905-1974), one of the first Tin Pan Alley songwriters. Jerome Kern wrote the melody. Ms. Fields wrote more than 400 songs for stage and film. Her father was a Polish immigrant who succeeded as a vaudeville comedian and Broadway producer. I suspect that she observed her father picking himself up many times and starting over on his way to success. "Pick Myself Up" became a popular tune in the 1930's and remains a jazz standard today. The song's hook is this: "I pick myself up, dust myself off, and start all over again." Maybe you should take a page from the Dorothy Fields playbook.

Believing that you are stuck is an illusion. Don't believe it. There is no such thing as stuck. You may have already made a decision that you don't like something in your life—like your work or a bad relationship—but the only real problem is your fear of change. Or you may need to make a major decision, but you feel you don't know enough to make it. A list of pros and cons won't help you if the number of pros is the same as the number of cons. Dilemmas are not responsible for your unwillingness to choose a course of action.

> Dr. Sheldon Kopp, author of *If You Meet the Buddha on the Road, Kill Him*, said that our most difficult life decisions have to be made with insufficient data. New York Yankee baseball star and manager Yogi Berra said, "When you come to a crossroads, take it."

While you need patience to make a wise decision, you have to be willing to jump. You may succeed, or you may learn something from failed efforts, but either is better than freezing or giving up.

As with other emotions, sad feelings are normal. I still grieve the loss of my parents, and the occasional wave of sadness reminds me of my good fortune in having had them. I wouldn't be sad if not for being so lucky. The sadness of loss wakes me to life's impermanence. It motivates me to make the best of my limited time and do some good while I am still on this planet.

If you suffer from ADHD and a co-existing depression, don't blame yourself. Get professional help if it is obstructing your daily functioning. Take medication if you need it. Wouldn't you wear eyeglasses if you needed them? Wouldn't you want to see as well as possible? You may be so accustomed to being told there is something wrong with you, that the suggestion of medical treatment may sound to you like criticism. Get over it! Your brain is like your other organs. It can malfunction. It can recycle a neurotransmitter too rapidly, and medication could regulate that.

There is much that you can do with or without medicine. You can become more aware of your negative self-talk. Human brains tend to gravitate toward negative thinking. This is because we have had to overcome obstacles and solve problems since the beginning of time. But tendencies are tendencies; we don't have to actualize them. Making room for positive thought requires intentional effort. We have to open our eyes to see possibilities and opportunities. We have to wake up to see the beauty that surrounds us. You may have noticed that some of the most touching acts of love have occurred in times of war and natural disasters.

Being aware of negative thoughts can help you practice circumventing them. If you carried around a checklist of the most common types, you would be surprised at how often you indulge them.

Here are twelve types of negative thoughts:

- Overgeneralizing—predicting negative outcomes because of one experience

- Disqualifying the positive—ignoring information that contradicts your negative view

- All or nothing thinking—it is all good or all bad, no middle ground

- Personalizing—taking responsibility for others' feelings. "It must be because of me."

- Catastrophizing—expecting an unbearable outcome

- Emotional reasoning—buying your feelings as truths

- Mind reading—assuming you know the thoughts and feelings of others

- Fortune telling—predicting a bad outcome

- Guilt beatings—inflexible thinking about what you should have done

- Magnifying/minimizing—overstating negative experiences and understating positive experiences

- Blaming—making others responsible for problems in your life

- Labeling—attaching a negative label to yourself or someone else

You don't have to memorize the list, or any list of negative thoughts. Such lists are widely available. In fact, you could just simply practice dropping judgment whenever you notice that you are judging. There is judgment in all of the so-called automatic negative thoughts described above. If you practiced fifteen minutes of meditation daily in which you responded to rising thoughts with, "Stop judging," you would see that almost every rising thought is evaluating something. Stepping away from such thoughts clears the mind, allowing you to simply observe non-judgmentally and see more clearly what is around you and within you.

A routine practice of mindfulness can sharpen your ability to observe angry thoughts, anxious thoughts, and negative thoughts. If you don't wake up to them, they can disproportionately influence your actions. You can more quickly recover your reasoning abilities when you skillfully observe your emotions, and notice how they influence your thoughts. This is called emotional intelligence. To be emotionally intelligent is to experience equanimity, which means balance in your feelings and thoughts. To be emotionally intelligent is to be wise.

Try this exercise: Get up ten minutes early tomorrow morning and sit in a quiet place, wherever you are least likely to be interrupted. Take a few deep breaths and then relax into your breath's own natural rhythm. Just let your breath breathe you, so to speak, gently and quietly. Direct your attention to the sensations of your breath as you inhale and exhale. Feel the air coming into your nostrils and then going out. If observing the sensations of your breath is not enough to hold your attention, you might try counting your breaths: "one" at the end of your inhale, "two" at the end of your exhale, etc., until you reach ten, and then start over at one.

When your mind starts to drift into thinking, just gently return your awareness to the sensations of breathing, or to counting your breaths. There is nothing wrong when your mind starts to chew on some thought again. Just step away from your thoughts as soon as you become aware of them.

Notice the difference between:

1. being *in* a thought

2. *observing* that you are thinking

Notice the difference between:

1. being *in* a feeling

2. *noticing the sensation* of a feeling

Continue to repeat this returning of your attention to your breath, and you will begin to observe the gradual subsiding of the spinning wheels of thought. You will become more alert to what is happening in the present moment. You will experience how your body feels. You will notice sounds that you are hearing. You will be aware of your surroundings. You will see the nature of your thoughts without getting attached to them. All of this is happening in the moment. It may feel as if time is slowing down. This gentle effort to let go of effort is what allows you sit peacefully in the present moment. The peace that comes from being fully present in one moment is accessible to you, right there where you are sitting. It doesn't matter that you have ADHD. In fact, you might observe the contrast between chaos and clarity more fully than someone who doesn't have ADHD.

Remember that awareness of self includes awareness of your reactions to others. In your daily life, practice using your enhanced awareness (from practicing meditation) by quieting your mind when listening to others. Notice the difference between (1) listening to your thoughts about what the other person is saying and (2) listening deeply to the other person without your assumptions and judgments.

KEY POINTS TO PONDER:

- No one wishes to have uncomfortable feelings. But wishing not to have them can cause worse problems than the feelings themselves.

- The notion that you must *resolve* or *get over* some feeling in order to act is self-defeating.

- Practicing the skill of "observing your feelings" non-judgmentally is essential to living well with your emotions.

- A simple meditation exercise, such as the one presented in this chapter, can help you quiet your mind and contribute to a deeper, more peaceful self-awareness and emotional intelligence.

QUESTIONS FOR REFLECTION:

- Do you have trouble inhibiting your actions when you are feeling very emotional? If so, how does that usually "play out" in your life?

- In what way do you personally identify with the story of Geraldo presented in this chapter?

- What is your reaction to the following statement? "Even life's pleasurable waves are impermanent, and being aware of that reality allows you to embrace joy more fully in happy times."

- What has been your experience with meditation versus medication, as a means of addressing your ADHD?

Chapter Ten

A Labor of Love:
Using the Tools in Your Toolbox

> "There is a fountain inside you.
> Don't walk around with an empty bucket "
> — *Rumi*

Writing this book has been a labor of love for me, and it will be even more pleasing to me if it contributes to your own labor of love. My wish is for your labor to include love of effort, commitment to your values, acceptance of yourself and others, and mindfulness in your relationships. You don't have infinite time to use your gifts—these tools—unless you think you will have a chance in another life. When a wise teacher was asked if he believed there is life after death, he answered something like this: "I'm more interested in the question of whether there is life *before* death."

Now, it's time for you to stop thinking and start doing. You have been reading words on pages, which will do you no good if the ideas in this book are nothing more than mental activity. So, how will you turn these ideas into actions? Please don't say you will "try." Trying is not the same as doing. I want you to experiment boldly. If what you do doesn't help you, try another way. This chapter includes some recommended books, websites, and other resources.

Let me translate the preceding chapters into some action words for you:

- Fly your freak flag. Embrace yourself as you are and let your light shine.

- If you want to be productive, take one step and then keep moving.

- Show interest when listening and respect for the listener when speaking.

- Don't get lost in a self-absorbed bubble. Be a considerate friend.

- Pull your head out! Unplug from devices and other objects of mindlessness.

- Create something. Practice a craft or hobby that can bring joy into your life.

- Don't take yourself too seriously. Lighten up about your screw-ups, and be quiet about your achievements.

- When derailed, do what successful people do: start again without devaluing yourself.

- Allow your feelings to rise and subside, and doubt your emotionally-reactive story lines.

If you do nothing else, at least do the easy things. For example, if you are a college student, always show up for class. Assignments and exams might be difficult, but showing up for class is easy. Show up for support group meetings, take medicine if you need it, practice mindfulness (sitting quietly is not difficult), eat real food instead of junk, choose a fun way to exercise, ask for help, read online articles on ADHD and health, and use the simplest organizational strategies and tools that will work for you. If you could use some help, seek out a life coach, ADHD coach, professional organizer, meditation teacher, mentor, psychotherapist, or psychiatrist. Don't let any stigma or shame get in the way of allowing help that you might need, or you may as well try to get comfortable with underachievement and difficult relationships. If living with your ADHD brain has always seemed hard, why not make it easier?

New ways to enhance your brain's functioning—both medical and non-medical—will continue to emerge, as sure as the sun rises. But none of them will serve you unless you choose to use your brain in new ways and do some good with it. A refurbished car in your garage can be like a trophy to show to guests, but it won't transport you anywhere unless you take it out of the garage and drive it. If your brain is wired for creativity, for example, it won't matter if you don't create anything. If you don't direct your attention to your priorities and sustain your effort, you will achieve little, and you won't be happy.

So here are some tools you can use to enhance your life, and hopefully, the lives of others that will be touched by yours:

About Medical Tools

If you take medicine for your ADHD and any co-existing conditions, keep in mind that the purpose of medicine is to level the playing field in order to be successful with developing skillful ways to manage your life and your relationships. Medicine makes a positive difference around 80 percent of the time and should be given serious consideration. Getting the best from medication usually means being patient enough to find the right medicine and the right dosage for you. If you are among the fortunate few, your life might improve dramatically with medicine alone. If you are among the majority, you have more work to do. Once you get the right medicine and dosage, focus your effort on the skills of living well rather than on perfecting medicine. The drug is not a cure. Think in terms of getting to a "best place" with medication so you can swallow the pill and forget about it. Think about your life instead.

A university professor, who was compulsively changing medications and dosages, trying incessantly to perfect his experience, became excessively focused on the medicine. He went back and forth between two types of stimulants, and up and down with the dosages of each. Eventually, I asked him if he could just let it be and stop compulsively searching for perfection. He acknowledged needing to give more of his attention to the life changes that he wanted to make.

> For a good overview of medicines and how they work, visit the website for the National Resource Center on ADHD (www.help4adhd.org).

Understand that you can take medication and still fail to direct your brain in any useful direction. I have seen many adolescents and young adults take medicine and then have their brains hijacked by their electronic devices just as much as before they took medicine.

If you are someone who dislikes the idea of taking medicine, ask your doctor about any concerns you have regarding its safety and possible side effects, and then consider giving it a trial run. After allowing enough opportunity to explore different medications and dosages as necessary, toss them if they don't help you.

If you find a medication that you tolerate well, don't panic if someone tells you that you are not your normal self. That might actually be a good thing! You may be like my clients who felt they were too serious after beginning medication, and believed they had lost their sense of humor. It is possible. But it is also possible that before medicine, they were indiscriminate about where and when they chose to express humor. Class clowns make some students laugh, but they annoy and disrupt others. And they get into trouble, just like you probably do with your spouse!

Still, if negative effects of medicine exceed the benefits, you might be better off without it. Anyone could have some undesirable experiences with medicine. Just remember that you could be taking the wrong medicine or the wrong dosage. People respond differently to them. Sometimes medicine that is prescribed for a co-existing condition can make ADHD symptoms worse. For example, if one of your medications makes you sleepy, it may compromise the effects of your ADHD medicine. But if your medicine ramps you up to where you feel jittery, your dosage may be too high. This is not a one-size-fits-all deal.

Determining if medicine is best for you is ultimately your call. You wouldn't let your optometrist tell you that lens number one is clearer than lens number two. She asks you to tell *her.*

Understand that how you *feel* when taking medicine is not the way to judge its effectiveness. Instead, you should evaluate medicine based on the reasons you got a diagnosis and a prescription in the first place—*observations of the symptoms of ADHD.* Enlisting a trusted friend or mate to help evaluate its effects is a good idea.

Use your web browser to search for the "ARS Symptom Checklist" to view the World Health Organization's international checklist of symptoms.

Non-medical Tools

While medication will likely make it much easier for you to develop new skills and habits, it docsn't just eliminate your ADHD symptoms. It won't teach you to:

- Keep track of your obligations
- Be considerate of others
- Prioritize effectively
- Activate on the most important tasks
- Use your creative potential
- Be a competent relationship partner
- Pull your head out of mindless distractions

Whatever activities you may find to improve your brain's functioning, remember that they are all paths and not destinations. You don't drive a well-built car just to be on the road, but to get somewhere. And your vehicle does not have to be perfect to transport you. A balanced and healthy lifestyle isn't a cure for ADHD, but as with anyone's brain and body, it will support improved functioning and get you somewhere.

If you are organizationally challenged, check out the National Association of Professional Organizers at www.napo.net to find a professional organizer near you, or go to their "virtual chapter" at www.napovc.com. They can help you organize your home or office and teach you how to maintain what you organize.

I have been inspired by many adults who allowed me to join them in observing their tendencies and behavior patterns through the lens of ADHD. Their responses enlightened me in two ways:

- They would say, "I never thought about it that way," and I realized that I had framed their behavior in a way that was new to them.

- They would say something that made me think, "I never thought about it that way," and I would realize that they had framed something in a way that was unique in my experience.

I was inspired to write a book that was more of a "perspective" than a "prescription." There are excellent prescription books and ADHD coaches already available. And there are authors who offer both (I recommend reading Zylowska, Orlov, Tuckman, Solden, Hallowell and Ratey, and Giwerc).

Before prescribing ways to develop new skills and use new strategies, I needed to help my clients with a way to understand, accept, and embrace their ADHD brains. And so I began with the question of who we are and who we are not. Years of living with the misperceptions of others—people who don't really get you—may have contributed to feeling like you don't know yourself.

Many clients over the years have asked me to help them with self-esteem, yet that is something I cannot give to anyone. Self-esteem is having an honest and accurate appraisal of your abilities and challenges, and accepting them all without judgment. Evaluating your *performance* has value, but judging the *self* creates an unnecessary and confusing problem: You don't know which one the self is. Is it the one that is judging, or the one that is being judged? There is only *one* of you. Judging the self creates an extra you that is not needed. You came into this world with value. You have it; you just need to act like you know it! And it is important to recognize that self-loathing serves nothing and no one. If your brain is different from the average brain, there is no reason not to accept it. In fact, it can be a good thing. All you need is the courage and willingness to be yourself.

If you have the opposite problem—too much regard for yourself—and live in a narcissistic bubble, you can learn how to practice humility and positive regard for others, and how to stop judging and manipulating others. There are mindfulness-based cognitive therapists and meditation teachers who can help with this. They can teach you compassion meditation exercises, which typically involve learning to direct compassion to oneself first before extending it to others. Giving to others is actually good for one's own physical and mental health.

> A wonderful resource for guided meditations—meditation for beginners, Zen meditation, compassion meditation, and many other forms of guided practice—can be found in the "Insight Timer" app that you can download on your smart phone or tablet. It includes many useful features—like reminders to meditate, bell timers, and a journal feature.
>
> An excellent series of guided meditations developed for adults with ADHD can be found on a CD in the back cover of Dr. Lidia Zylowska's book, *The Mindfulness Prescription for Adult ADHD*. The book is a great resource too, as is her MP3 album (www.lidiazylowska.com).
>
> An easily accessible resource for beginning a mindfulness practice, tailored for adults with ADHD, can be found at www.mindfullyadd.com.

You can learn to be a competent relationship partner, which will reward both you and your partner. You must understand, accept, and be willing to regard the effects that your ADHD has on your relationship. There is expertise available to you today to help with this. If you need the help of a therapist, be sure it is someone with expertise on ADHD and knowledge of its effects on relationships. Don't be afraid to decline a therapist and keep looking until you find the best fit for your needs. Apart from therapy, there are workshops and classes available for couples dealing with ADHD in their marriage, along with some excellent books.

> Melissa Orlov is the ADHD-marriage expert, and her website has it all. You will find her books, blog, forum, treatment guides, and information on her classes for couples—a wealth of information in English and Spanish—at www.adhdmarriage.com. Orlov is the author of *The ADHD Effect on Marriage* and co-author with Nancie Kohlenberger of *The Couple's Guide to Thriving with ADHD.*
>
> John Gottman, PhD, offers researched-based information in his books and workshops on what makes marriages work, and what makes them fail (www.gottman.com). He is the author of many useful books, including *The Seven Principles for Making Marriage Work* and *What Makes Love Last?*

If you want to get things done, you will need to practice activating. Just "wash one dish." Throw yourself mindfully into one simple part of the task, as if it is all you have to do, and you won't feel overwhelmed. To sustain your effort, keep moving forward and notice—without judgment—your inclination to stop and do something else. An inclination is not a problem. Just pause briefly and then return your attention to the task at hand, as often as necessary. This is mindfulness in real time, where it counts. Continue this practice for about a month or two and you will have formed a new habit, which is a brain change. Completion of a task is inherently rewarding; you just need to get to the finish line to experience the reward.

Forget memory! If your memory is unreliable, why rely on it? Use another tool from your toolbox to keep track of obligations. The memory in your electronic devices may be more reliable than your brain's ability to park and retrieve information. And if you simply prefer the broader display of ink on paper, your calendar may be a more reliable tool. I find that a printed calendar with a view of an entire week is more useful than the calendar in my smart phone, where out of site is out of mind.

Cultivate your creative potential, and don't believe for a moment that you are not creative. Chances are, you have unlearned that you are creative, especially if you have had sufficient experience being criticized and pressured to conform. Neuroscientist Allan Reiss, MD is quoted in the Stanford Medicine News Center, saying researchers at Stanford "found that activation of the brain's executive-control centers—the parts of the brain that enable you to plan, organize, and manage your activities—is negatively associated with creative task performance" (www.med.stanford.edu, May 28, 2015). Neuropsychologist, Rex Jung, PhD, another expert studying creativity at the University of New Mexico, said in a National Public Radio interview that "less is best" when it comes to creativity. He explained that less executive activity allows for more free interplay among various parts of the brain. That interplay, he said, is associated with creativity (www.rexjung.com). Well, guess what? ADHD brains have less than average executive activity as a rule. I compare this phenomenon to having the parent take a break from directing the children's activity and allowing them to play. So, if you have this creative potential, I would recommend that you use it!

Remember that you are not born with the knowledge base and skill you will need in order to create something. Potential becomes creative activity only with directed effort, and effort means learning and practicing. With dedicated effort, creative people often outperform less creative people with higher IQ scores.

Be skillful in managing your emotional life. You were born with all the emotions you need to survive and adapt. So you should respect your feelings, their adaptive function, and their historical roots. But don't allow your feelings to run your life. Don't believe the story lines that your emotions want you to believe. Keep an open mind, a "beginner's mind," and keep your reasoning brain online and in charge, regardless of momentary feelings and impulses.

You can learn more about emotion regulation in two of my favorite books on the subject and my favorite workbook for learning and practicing it: *The Emotional Life of Your Brain* by Richard Davidson, PhD, and Sharon Begley (www.richardjdavidson.com), *Emotional Chaos to Clarity* by Phillip Moffitt (www.dharmawisdom.org), and the workbook, *Get Out of Your Mind and Into Your Life*, by Steven Hayes, PhD (www.stevenchayes.com).

Life is a precious gift. Live well with your ADHD by managing your life skillfully, and do some good with your gift. If your intentions and efforts are in line with your values and goals, your life's work will be a labor of love. And managing your life will be rewarding because it will allow your creative brain to serve you, and others, in personally important ways.

Appendix

Starting and Leading an ADHD Support Group

How can you use your exceptional capacity and your creativity to achieve excellence? I presented this question in an ADHD support group meeting one evening. The topic, which was posted in advance, drew a full house. We usually have a good turnout when the topic is related to strengths. What follows are some points that participants offered to one another. Some of the names have been changed to protect privacy.

Margaret acknowledged being hyperactive, but she likes her energy. She refuses to allow her voice to be silenced. Throughout her life, people often told her, "You can't do that," or "You can't do it that way." There was a time when those voices had become her own. She had learned to censor herself and not regard her creative potential. And then she read a book entitled *Ignore Everybody: And 39 Other Keys to Creativity* by Hugh Macleod. She told the support group that she has learned to ignore everybody who would judge her while she is *in the process of creating*. Ignoring everybody, she said, is what creative people do when they are creating.

When Connie finished writing her book, she had no desire to celebrate. There was no more urgency or novelty in that project. She was done, and it was time to start the next project. She attributed her successful completion of the book to her ability to hyperfocus. Individuals with ADHD can achieve excellence by taking advantage of that ability. "We overcomplicate things," Connie told the group. "Instead of always feeling like something is missing, we need to feel whole. When we accept that we are whole, we naturally create." Connie believes that we will not see the extraordinary in ourselves until we stop the negative self-talk.

Nate was sketching faces on his tablet throughout the meeting, but it was evident that he was tuned in to the discussion. His comments were pertinent. He had discovered that pursuing his passion for drawing made him happy. He rejected the suggestion from peers that he could earn income with his ability to draw.

Nate didn't wish to do it for income, he said, but to satisfy his need to create. He is happiest when he maintains that perspective. He has a regular 9-to-5 job that pays him well enough. When he creates to satisfy himself, he sustains his effort and enjoys his life. He said it helps to have a support network that encourages him.

Phil is on the very high functioning end of the autism spectrum. He is remarkably intelligent, but he has trouble reading people. Until recently, he believed that how he thought was no different from how everyone else thought. "I think in patterns," he said. He wondered why so many people weren't smart enough to do simple tasks or learn languages quickly. He didn't think he was particularly intelligent, but was puzzled as to why others struggled with what came easily to him. Now he recognizes that his brain's default mode of "thinking in patterns" has given him extraordinary abilities. One example is how easily he learns languages. Classroom lectures and textbooks did not help him, he said. When asked what message he wanted to convey to his ADHD peers from his experience, Phil suggested that each one of us needs to be more in touch with our uniqueness.

These brief interactions exemplify the richness of a support group. Almost everyone who comes for the first time either tells the group, or tells me privately, that they felt validated by being in the room with so many like-minded people. As one young man said to the group at the end of his first meeting: "This is my tribe!"

Mistakes to Avoid When Starting a Support Group

Failing to Lead

Like many individuals with ADHD, I learn *after* jumping in and making mistakes. I have trouble stepping outside of *now* and conceptualizing *future*. I will be pleased if sharing my early mistakes helps spawn new support groups that avoid my mistakes.

I am grateful for the early, pioneering members who once called me to task for having wasted the group's precious time. One evening I allowed someone to dominate the meeting with complaints about a family problem that had nothing to do with ADHD. I was tired that night, having rushed from my last psychotherapy appointment, and was not leading. Two members cornered me after the meeting. They rightfully challenged me for letting someone hijack the group, and they insisted that I do something about it. I began to be more active in leading and trying to keep us on track. Still, the changes that followed were insufficient. Keeping the group on topic wasn't enough, especially when there was no topic to begin with. The group needed a way to protect itself from itself. Unmanaged ADHD in a group process can be self-defeating.

Too Much Introducing

I had to stop introductions at the beginning of meetings, except for welcoming newcomers. I had been asking each person to give their name and speak briefly about their most difficult challenge with ADHD. Assuming that everyone could speak briefly was a mistake. The first introduction would be brief. And then, as we continued around the circle, participants would become increasingly comfortable. They not only introduced themselves and their particular challenge, they had stories to tell. Introductions turned into a storytelling festival. When I reminded the group that we were still introducing ourselves, someone would say, "Oh yes," and the introductions would resume until someone derailed the process again with story time.

At the end of an hour and a half of "introductions," there was no time left for anything else. It was like an evening at The Comedy Store—fun, but not productive. So now, we just welcome new people and jump into the work, which begins with the leader introducing the topic announced in advance by email.

Since we don't remember each other's names from one week to the next, one dedicated member took on the responsibility of creating nicely printed nametags for everyone. He keeps them all in an alphabetized file box and hands them out at the beginning of each meeting. Each nametag is inserted into a plastic cover that hangs from a string necklace. We have well over 200 first names on the tags, and we keep blank ones to make new tags for new members as they arrive. The average attendance is about sixteen participants.

Sixteen People + No Topic = Chaos

Without enough structure and active leadership, a group can waste time and lose valuable participants. When I considered having a topic in each meeting, I worried that an ADHD group might not tolerate the imposition of a topic and being held to it. I was wrong. Experience demonstrated that centering the group's collective attention at the outset was easier than trying to rescue the group from chaos. Returning the group's attention provided a corrective learning opportunity—a guided mindfulness exercise, in effect. Announcing the topic in advance, by email notifications, stimulates interest. Notifications are easily managed through our Yahoo Groups site (addnashville@yahoogroups.com) and my website (terrymhuff.com).

No Purpose, No Compass

I once experimented with having one of the two monthly meetings dedicated to learning about meditation and practicing it. I had been insisting that a routine practice of mindfulness was important for us and felt the need to do more than talk about it. But an entire meeting dedicated to meditation, leaving just one monthly meeting for support and strategies, didn't work. It was too much of one and too little of the other, and we lost participants.

Before abandoning the idea altogether, we experimented with shorter meditation practices in one of the two monthly meetings. The consensus was to practice meditating for twenty minutes at the beginning, discuss the experience and ways to enhance our mindfulness practices, and end with another twenty minutes of meditation. The first time we implemented our plan, a newcomer arrived late and sat next to me. She missed most of the instructions. Trying to catch on to what we were about to begin, she whispered to me, "Do you mean we are just going to sit here and do nothing for twenty minutes?" I replied, "Yes, that's about right." Regretfully, I never saw her again after that meeting, and we abandoned the idea after that night.

Keep it Interesting

Years before founding ADDNashville, I attended two support group meetings elsewhere. ADHD was a newly recognized disorder then. On both occasions there was an invited speaker. I found it almost impossible to stay tuned to the speakers, having worked all day and not eaten dinner. Although the first speaker was interesting—a speech and hearing professional who spoke about similarities between ADHD and central auditory processing disorder—I was distracted by the irony of trying to process information about why I was having trouble processing. When I arrived late to my second meeting, I learned that a scheduled speaker had not shown, and the leader chose to be the substitute speaker for the evening. He was a nice man, and I respected his commitment. But I needed a different kind of challenge from trying to sit still and listen while tired and hungry. I didn't return.

After my own experiments and mistakes, I concluded that participants needed advance notice of a topic, and needed to participate actively from the outset of each meeting. And the group needed to be managed. Unmanaged, the risk of losing focus and losing members was too high. Someone would interrupt, another would have a conversation with the person next to him. Someone would lose awareness of others when telling a personal story, or the opposite would happen: someone would have difficulty seizing an opportunity to speak. So I developed guidelines for participation, which you will find at the end of this appendix. To readers who were in those early group meetings, I beg your forgiveness and embrace the lessons you taught me. To those who endured the early years and remained, I am grateful for your commitment and leadership. You helped us mature into a group that supports and challenges us.

Tips for Starting a Support Group

My view of an effective support group for adults with ADHD is one in which:

- Everyone feels they have a place at the table, a place where they will be welcomed and valued.

- Participants feel that they are not alone with their experiences and that others can understand them.

- They get to see that ADHD grows up in different homes with different family histories, and they have different aspirations and careers.

- Participants experience diversity within the "family." They are alike in many important ways, and yet no one participant is like another.

- The group protects itself from its collective inattention by guidelines to avoid diversions, interruptions, and distractions.

- Strengths are highlighted and honored.

- Individuals share strategies and tools that have proven helpful to them.

- Success stories are celebrated and the pain of loss is shared.

- The primary focus is learning to live well with the brains we have.

Understanding ADHD, understanding one another, and being mutually supportive would become essential features of our group, and the primary focus would be perspective, strategies, and tools. The degree of mutual support that I observed early in the life of our group was an unanticipated and rewarding experience. Participants have demonstrated remarkable sensitivity to the pain that their peers have experienced from living with ADHD. My observations contradicted any notion that adults with ADHD are incapable of empathy. *ADHD is not a deficit of empathy.* Sincere compassion comes from knowing the pain of being misunderstood, disregarded, disrespected, ridiculed, rejected, and berated. The group's sensitivity keeps participants returning and expressing gratitude for having this community of ADHD peers. When one participant's mother had a stroke, the group displayed a degree of compassion and respect that one might expect from biological relatives.

One evening, someone raised a provocative question at the end of the meeting: Are adults with ADHD incapable of love? Responders were respectful toward the member who raised the question, but most felt the answer was "no." Still, his pain was not lost on them, and their concern for him was evident. The question touched a personal chord with one participant who responded eloquently to the individual who posed the question. What can easily be mistaken for lacking capacity for love, he proposed, is just "episodic inattention." That useful response was the kind of contribution that points us in some direction. We can do something about episodic inattention, but not inability to empathize.

When I first thought of starting an ADHD support group, I sought out information about what others had done. I was never good at reading and following directions, but I found some material about how to organize a support group. One booklet suggested creating a board, establishing committees, and writing by-laws. I could not imagine organizing a board and writing by-laws. The thought of it was so unappealing that I almost gave up my idea of starting a group. I decided to do what my daughter once did when she was five years old: I would throw some mud against the wall and see what would stick.

Most of the good ideas for running a support group did not spring from within me. I have been fortunate to have a lot of creative minds around me. I surveyed potential participants in my startup meeting to determine how best to structure the group, and to decide what its focus should be. A university professor, knowledgeable about group processes, encouraged me to consider my own goals and preferences. "This is your group," he reminded me. "It should reflect some of your own values. What you want it to be," he told me, "is no less important than the input from others."

I was clear about what I did *not* want. I was not going to create a "whiner's group." I would not be able to tolerate complaints about how awful it is to be cursed with this disorder, and it would not be useful. What I wanted was a group that would encourage experimentation and creativity. I wanted participants to be confident enough to fly their freak flags proudly, a group that embraced diversity and accepted eccentricity. I wanted to see participants share ideas, strategies, tools, books, websites, and other resources. I wanted to see them understand, support, and encourage each other. I preferred to have a little fun and make it appealing enough for people to come at an hour when they normally might be eating dinner or watching television.

Occasionally, we will have "professional guests" join us. We don't have speakers because we don't have listeners! Professional guests are told in advance that they should talk for no more than twenty minutes about what they do, and then they can join our discussion. If participants want to use all of the remaining time to ask questions of the guests and discuss their work, they can. But once guests have presented, they are participants in the group process. We do not allow guests to market products and services. The focus is always on serving participants.

Individuals with ADHD are not particularly fond of rules. In fact, we are inclined to be oppositional and defiant. In the early years I would not consider imposing rules on the group, but then I observed negative effects of insufficient structure. Frequently, a participant would follow someone's contribution with a story that had nothing to do with what the speaker had said. Sometimes the group seemed not to notice the derailment, and they would follow the leader right down the winding trail. Whenever I redirected the group's attention back to the original speaker's comment, participants seemed abruptly awakened to what happened. Returning to the topic mimicked returning to the breath in meditation. There are learning effects when this kind of redirection happens—an unplanned experience of drifting to mindlessness and returning to mindfulness—which illustrates the value of active leadership. I believe participants are grateful when the original thread of communication is recovered. Collective ADHD is not that different from individual ADHD. We need protection from our own habitual tendencies to digress, distract, and interrupt.

The question of how often to meet was challenging for me. Weekly was too often for my schedule, and monthly was too infrequent for the needs of the group. Leading a support group is a big commitment, and leaders have to consider their own time while also considering the needs of the group. If you are unlikely to sustain a routine of weekly meetings over the long haul, because of your other commitments, then you should meet less often. Otherwise, you will burn out. But if you meet too infrequently, your members might not have sufficient opportunity to develop relationships and maintain a collective identity.

After we abandoned efforts to designate one of the two monthly meetings to meditation practice, we tried a two-minute period of silence aimed at beginning the meetings with mindfulness and acceptance—of themselves and each other. At first, we encountered a problem with participants coming in late. We addressed it by posting a sign on the door at the beginning to inform late arrivers that a two-minute meditation was in process. Latecomers would have to wait in the hallway until the door was opened for them. The two minutes of silence was helpful to the productivity of our meetings, and it encouraged mindfulness practices at home. It also had the unexpected effect of encouraging members to arrive on time. Maintaining routines can be difficult for us. Still, sustaining effort comes with recurring practice and payoff, the same as any other habit.

Finally, we had to address how to keep track of participants. At the beginning I had an outdated method for keeping up with email addresses and reminding participants of meetings. Then one member suggested a simple Yahoo Groups site that could send automatic reminders for meetings to members, and allow the group leader to inform participants of topics in advance. Eric—

a resourceful member who knows how these things work—
arranged for two reminders, one of them arriving three days before
a meeting and the other on the day of the meeting.

It became clear over time that we needed more structure to
protect ourselves from ourselves. I developed guidelines so we
could adhere to the group's purpose and be productive. I chose
not to refer to the structure as "rules" because of our inherent
aversion to rules. Our "guidelines" evolved over the course of a
few months.

Guidelines for ADDNashville Support Group Participation

These guidelines are intended to help us prevent lapses in
mindfulness—and the challenges of being a large group—from
interfering with a balanced process in our discussions. I want all
participants, especially newcomers, to feel safe and encouraged to
contribute. Our 90-minute meeting provides us an opportunity to
practice being mindful of others, to become good listeners, and
to practice shifting between open awareness and focused
attention. Although we may speak clearly and listen attentively
when focused, we also need to practice shifting to open awareness
and remain mindful of the group as a whole, the passing of time,
and the balance of participation. I will appreciate your efforts
to help keep this group working effectively and efficiently for
all participants.

1. Please do not interrupt the speaker.

2. Speakers, please be mindful that others want time to
   speak as well.

3. Practice being a good listener.

4. Please do not offer advice unless the speaker asks for it.

5. Speakers, feel free to indicate that you would like
   suggestions; otherwise, we will assume that you are not
   requesting advice.

---

6. Please avoid long autobiographical stories, and try not to repeat personal stories you have already shared. We can get lost in our stories and lose awareness of the group.

7. If you can't get a word in, feel free to signal the group with your hands. If that doesn't work, you may try any creative means to get the group's attention.

8. Please do not carry on a conversation with the person next to you during our 90 minutes. Address the group instead.

9. Please be respectful of privacy. It is okay to tell others generally what we talk about, but do not share specifics of someone's personal experience. And please respect that individual members might not want to be identified as participants in a support group.

10. Please silence your phones and put your electronic devices away during the meeting, except when looking up something pertinent to the discussion. (Doodling will be tolerated for those who focus better when fidgeting!).

11. Please make every effort to arrive on time. Be respectful of new participants who remain time-challenged and those whose schedules prevent them from arriving at 6:30.

Some Tips for Starting

Chances are, if you are starting a support group, you are in the ADHD family. You may have ADHD, or you have a partner or child with ADHD. You don't have to be an expert to start a group, but you will need a knowledge base about the ADHD brain and about group process. You will need to be mindful of the difference between opinions and facts, between myths and realities, and between assumptions and truths. You should know if what you are reading or hearing is an opinion, a widely held belief, an anecdotal observation, or a research-based fact. You will have to speak up and dispel myths and inaccurate assumptions; otherwise, your silence may inadvertently lend credibility to incorrect notions.

You must lead with genuine respect. Everyone has a place at the table. That doesn't mean that you should allow someone's negativity or disruptive tendencies to derail the group. But challenges to any individual in the presence of others should be presented sensitively. Being respectful and sensitive doesn't mean being afraid to risk offending in order to take care of the group. That is difficult for me, but necessary. There will be times when you may need to give feedback privately. Individuals with ADHD are not always aware of their negative effect on the group. But be mindful also that approaching someone outside the group can backfire, as it can make an issue seem more serious than if addressed sensitively in the group. The leader must balance being respectful of individual members, their ADHD, and the integrity of the group.

You *must* manage the group. One disastrous meeting can drive away the most sensitive and compassionate members. If you tend to be exhausted from work on the day of meetings, then you may want to arrange your schedule so you aren't working right up until the meeting time. I started designating our meeting day as a day when I would not see clients in the afternoon. Except when I violate my own rule and see a late client on Monday, I have much more energy for leading actively.

You are the *guide* for a support group. You are not a group therapist. It is important to know the difference. You are guiding the interactions among distractible and impulsive individuals. Your job is to watch the process and make sure that it is serving the group. You are also a participant. While you should have expertise, you cannot be a know-it-all. You would not want to discourage others from researching and presenting new information. Some participants will cruise websites, read books, attend online seminars, and otherwise find information valuable to the group. Such generosity and commitment is honorable.

Inform yourself of resources in the community. Individuals with ADHD usually need a community of support that can include ADHD coaches, professional organizers, psychotherapists, psychiatrists, financial advisors, life coaches, career counselors, and educational resources. It is important not to allow group members to advise one another about specific doctors or medicines. One person's experience of a provider or medicine is just one person's experience. A participant once discouraged anyone from taking a particular medicine. He had experienced horrible side effects with it. "Don't ever take that drug," he told participants. Others responded that the same medicine was the only one that ever helped them. Likewise, one person may relate to one physician or therapist better than another.

You will need to network with other professionals in the community. They will be among the best sources of referrals to the group and may have some good ideas for topics. My group is publicized mostly by word of mouth through professional networking, my website, local and national organizations' websites, the website of the church where we meet, and members telling others in their own social and work circles.

If you want to start a support group, don't try to do everything by yourself. Seek out some like-minded individuals, including at least one professional with expertise in ADHD, and at least one non-ADHD person who likes organizing and structuring. But don't think it has to be perfect from the start, or else you will never start.

Notes

1. Eve M. Valera, Stephen V. Farone, Kate E. Murray, and Larry J. Seidman, "Meta-Analysis of Structural Imaging Findings in Attention-Deficit/Hyperactivity," *Biological Psychiatry,* June, 2006.

2. Seung Sahn, *The Compass of Zen*, Shambhala Publications, Inc., 1977.

3. Harry Chapin, "Flowers Are Red," from the album *Living Room Suite,* Warner Communications, Inc., 1978.

4. Shunryu Suzuki, *Zen Mind*, Beginner's Mind, Weatherhill, Inc., 1986.

5. Lidia Zylowska, *The Mindfulness Prescription for Adult ADHD*, Shambhala Publications, 2012.

6. Daniel Siegel, *The Mindful Brain*, W. W. Norton & Company, Inc., 2007.

7. Brenda Ueland, *Tell Me More: On the Fine Art of Listening*, Kore Press, 1998.

8. Melissa Orlov, *The ADHD Effect on Marriage*, Specialty Press, Inc., 2010.

9. Carly Simon, "Anticipation," Warner Music Group, NY, 1971.

10. Jill Bolte Taylor, *My Stroke of Insight*, Plume, 2009.

11. Connie Williams, *Thinking Consciously Rocks*, Nashville Advertising & Promotions, Inc., 2012.

12. Terry Cole-Whitaker, *What You Think of Me Is None of My Business,* Oak Tree Publications, 1979.

13. Holly White and Priti Shah, "Creative Style and Achievement in Adults with Attention-Deficit/Hyperactivity Disorder," *Personality and Individual Differences,* volume 50, Issue 5, April 2011, 673-677.

14. Barry Scott Kauffman, "Beautiful Minds," *Psychology Today,* Feb. 27, 2011.

15. Paul Zollo, *Songwriters on Songwriting,* Forth Edition, Da Capo Press, 2003.

16. Marshall M. Rosenberg, *We Can Work It Out,* Puddle Dancer Press, 2004.

Index

A

acceptance, 77
acceptance and commitment therapy (ACT), 97-98
accepting your differences, 19
ACT. *See* acceptance and commitment therapy
activating
    and motivation, 11-12
    new and interesting projects, 22
    prioritizing, 14
    strategies for, 14
    you attention, 10
ADD and Loving It (video), 74
Adderall, 3
ADDNashville, 124-125, 130-131
ADHD
    accepting your differences, 19
    affect on behavior, 13
    anatomy of an ADHD brain, 3
    co-existing with depression, 104
    creating your environment for, 59
    and defining who you are, 1
    with depression, 104, 106
    educating others about, 74
    international checklist of symptoms, 115
    joy and pain of living with, 70
    labels ascribed to people with, 1, 4
    pattern in ADHD couples, 43-44
    responses to jokes about, 74-77
    symptoms of, 1-2
    tips for making a partnership work, 45-46
ADHD Effect on Marriage, The (Orlov), 42-43
admitting responsibility, 44
"After the Fire is Gone" (song), 39
alcohol use, 57-58
all or nothing thinking, 107
anger
    affect on relationships, 44-45
    and emotional intelligence, 97
    impulsive, 103
"Anticipation" (song), 55
anxiety. *See* emotions
arousal
    anxious, 101
    and overreactions, 70

ARS Symptom Checklist, 115
Artists Way, The (Cameron), 8
Astaire, Fred, 105
attention management
    and ADHD, 5
    and awareness, 50
    being in "the zone," 49
    described, 48
awareness
    of awareness, 26
    breathing exercise for, 108-109
    of the inclination to spin, 50
    of self, 109
    shifting between focused and open states, 6
awareness training, 32

B

Begley, Sharon, 120
behavior, ADHD affect on, 13
Berra, Yogi, 105
boredom, 15-16
brain chemistry, 3
brainlock, 52-53
breathing exercise, 108-109
the Buddha, 67
bullying, 75

C

Cameron, Julia, 8
Candy, John, 31
catastrophizing, 107
challenge, defining yours, 19
chaos, 124
Chapin, Harry, 8-9
Chappell, Jim, 65
coffee as medication, 88
communication. *See also* listening
    being defensive and, 6, 26-27
    with bullies, 75
    in conflict, 103
    golden rule of, 29
    harsh speech, 34-35
    mindful speaking, 26, 30-34
    nonverbal signals, 24
    nonviolent, 103
    self-talk, 12, 106
    through criticism, 87
    through posture, 27

Reader's Notes